Architecture and Implementation
of
Large Scale IBM Computer Systems

ALSO FROM Q.E.D.

MANAGEMENT

Strategic Planning for Information Systems, R.V. Head.
Managing for Productivity in Data Processing, J.R. Johnson.
Effective Methods of EDP Quality Assurance, W.E. Perry.
Managing Systems Maintenance, W.E. Perry.
A Guide to EDP Performance Management, D.P. Norton & K.G. Rau.
The Handbook for Data Center Management, R. Kinderlehrer.
The Data Center Disaster Consultant, K.W. Lord, Jr.
Handbook for Data Processing Educators, R. Sullivan.

TECHNICAL

Computer Control and Audit, W.C. Mair, D.W. Wood, & K.W. Davis.
Human Factors in Office Automation, W.O. Galitz.
Handbook of Screen Format Design, W.O. Galitz.
Architecture and Implementation of Large Scale IBM Computer Systems,
    N.S. Prasad.
Structured Requirements Definition, K. Orr.
1001 Questions and Answers to Help You Prepare for the CDP® Exam,
    K. Lord.
Handbook of COBOL Techniques, Computer Partners, Inc.
Microcomputer Buyer's Guide, T. Webster.
Advances in Computer System Security, R. Turn, ed.

DATA BASE

Data Base Management Systems, L.J. Cohen.
Creating and Planning the Corporate Data Base System Project, L.J. Cohen.
Data Base Techniques, BIS Applied Systems, Ltd.
IMS Design and Implementation Techniques, T.J. McElreath.
Design Guide for CODASYL Data Base Management Systems, R. Perron.
The Data Base Monograph Series, R.M. Curtice, ed., 9 reports.
Data Base Systems: A Practical Reference, I.A. Palmer.
Data Dictionary Systems, H.C. Lefkovits.

TELECOMM/DATA COMM

Dimension PBX and Alternatives, Economics & Technology, Inc.
CTMS Adviser, Economics & Technology, Inc.
Transnational Data Regulation: The Realities, Online Conferences, Ltd.
Distributed Processing: Current Practice and Future Developments, Expertise
    International, Ltd.
Telecommunications in the U.S.: Trends and Policies, L. Lewin, ed.
Advances in Computer Communications and Networking, W.W. Chu, ed.

WRITE FOR A FREE CATALOG

Architecture and Implementation
of
Large Scale IBM Computer Systems

N.S. Prasad

Vice President
IMI Systems, Inc.
New York City

Q.E.D. Information Sciences, Inc.
Wellesley, Massachusetts

ARCHITECTURE AND IMPLEMENTATION OF LARGE
SCALE IBM COMPUTER SYSTEMS

Printed in the United States of America

Library of Congress Catalog Card Number: 81-85893

International Standard Book Number: 0-89435-051-X

Table of Contents

FIGURE CREDITS

The author and publisher gratefully acknowledge permission of the International Business Machines Corporation to reproduce a number of figures which appear in this volume. The figures, which are copyrighted by IBM, and their sources are listed below:

Figure 2-7, from "IBM System/370: Processors," (GA-22-7001-9), page 3-2, Figure 3-2.

Figure 5-2, ibid., page 2-1, Figure 2-1.

Figure 5-3, modified from Table 10-20.1, p. 53, "A Guide to the IBM 3033 Processor Complex, etc.," GC20-1859-5.

Figure 8-9, modified from Figure 2-6, p. 2-9, "OS/VS2 System Overview," GC 28-0984-1, 1980.

Figure 8-15, modified from Figure 1, page 2, "IBM 3031, 3032, and 3033 Processor Complex Channel Configuration Guidelines," GG 22-9020-00, 1978.

Figure 8-19, modified from "IBM System/370 Model 168 Functional Characteristics," GA 22-7010-6, 1979, Figure 5, page 11.

Figure 9-1, modified from Figure 3-1, page 3-1, "IBM 3081 Functional Characteristics" GA 22-7076-0, 1980.

Figure 10-5, modified from Figure 3, p. 9, "Systems 360 I/O Interface Introduction - Student Self-Study Course," SR 25-5202-5, 1970.

Figure 10-6, ibid., Figure 8, p. 39.

Figure 10-7, ibid., Figure 5, p. 29.

Figure 11-1, from p. 11, Figure 3, "Introduction to Advanced Communications Function," GC 30-3033-0, 1976.

Figure 11-2, ibid., p. 22, Figure 10.

Figure 11-3, from Figure 1-1, page 1-7, "IBM 3600 Finance Communication System Summary," GC 27-0001-8, 1979.

Figure 11-4, Figure 1, page 17, "IBM 8100 Information System Distributed Office Support Facility General Information," GC 27-0546-1, 1981.

Figure 11-9, from page 3-12, "IBM Synchronous Data Link Control: General Information," GA 27-3093-1, 1975.

Figure 11-14, from Figure J.3, page 74, "IBM 3704 and 3705 Communications Controllers Hardware," Student Text.

Figure 11-15, from Figure J.4, page 76, "IBM 3704 and 3705 Communications Controllers Hardware," Student Text.

Figure 11-18, from Figure 1.13, page 1-17, "IBM 3270 Operation and Design," Independent Study Program, 1978.

Preface

This book is written with a view to explain how large scale IBM computer systems work. The first part of the book is an exposition of the 370 architecture which is the basis of IBM large scale computer systems. Models such as the IBM 370/158, 370/168, 303X (X = 1,2,3) and 3081 all use the same architecture even though they differ considerably in implementation details. The second part of the book deals with the details of implementation of the IBM 3033, 370/168 and 3081. The units that perform instruction fetching and execution, cache memories, translation look-aside buffers and storage-interleaving are some of the topics that are discussed in this context. The third part of the book deals with the implementation of input/output subsystems, with special emphasis on communication subsystems and mass-storage subsystems. Some of the topics discussed in this respect are the 3705 Communications Controller, 3270 Information Display System, and the 3350 disk storage units. Both shared and non-shared configurations are discussed as well as the sequence of interactions between channel, control unit and device.

The author is greatly indebted to Robert Forman, president of IMI Systems, Inc. for his support and encouragement; also to Julie Daniels of IMI Systems, Inc. for assistance in preparation of the original manuscript which was typed with unflagging cheerfulness by Lori Noah, Joyce Andrews and Cynthia Conti. Fred Pearl went over the manuscript and made several valuable suggestions and the author owes him a lot for his insightful comments regarding several topics covered in this book. Finally, grateful acknowledgements are due to the publishing group of Q.E.D. Information Sciences under Mark Walsh for their competent professional help in putting the book together.

PART I
IBM 370 ARCHITECTURE

1. Introduction and Overview

A computer system consists of several interacting components, namely one or more central processing units, main storage, data channels and peripheral units. The architecture of the system specifies the functions of the components and the rules of interaction among the various components. The architecture also presents a unified approach for handling diversity among individual members of a given type of component; for example, input/output operations pertaining to diverse peripheral units such as a disk and a terminal are architecturally handled in exactly the same way. The implementation of components can vary within limits set by the architecture. For instance, two disk drives may perform the functions specified by the architecture but each may differ from the other in implementation features such as rotational position sensing or multiple track operations. Likewise, two central processing units can have the same architecture but their implementations can be different in such details as the size of the cache memory, the pipe-lining of operations and other parameters.

The objectives of this book are (1) to present the architecture used in large scale IBM computer systems (e.g., 370/168, 3033) which is known as the 370 architecture (2) to give case histories of implementation of large scale processors, specifically the IBM 370/168, 3033 and 3081 and (3) to describe the implementation of control units and devices used for I/O operations, specifically in respect to communication and direct access storage.

The 370 architecture is described in detail in the document "IBM System/370 Principles of Operation" which deals with the following topics:

o   the functional elements of a computer system, namely main storage, central processing unit (CPU), channels, control units and devices.

o   the set of rules or protocols for the interaction be-
    tween the various functional elements.

o   the set of instructions that can be executed by the
    CPU.

o   the sub-elements within each functional element that
    are required to process the specified instruction set
    (e.g., subchannels within channels).

The architecture uses a conceptual model of a computer
comprising the following elements:

o   CPU

o   Main Storage

o   Channels

o   Control Units

o   Devices

The interconnection between these elements is schematically illustrated in Figure 1-1. The CPU reads from or
writes to main storage during program execution and also
issues I/O instructions to channels pertaining to data
transfer between device and main storage. The channel
transfers data between a device and main storage via a
control unit and, on completion, notifies the CPU by means
of an I/O interruption.

This architectural model is similar to the model used by
the System 360, which is the percursor of the System 370.
The 370 architecture, however, superimposes the following
major additional functions on the 360 architecture,
namely:

o   use of virtual addresses by programs and the transla-
    tions of such addresses into real storage addresses.

o   use of multiple CPUs sharing the same memory to provide multiprocessing capability.

o   use of block multiplexer channels for interleaving I/O operations on direct access storage devices.

Furthermore, the 370 architecture is geared for the efficient functioning of a multiprogramming operating system like the MVS operating system. In order to gain a better understanding of the interaction between computer architecture and operating system functions, we have included as an appendix the concepts used in the design of the MVS operating system.   The reader would benefit most by consulting this appendix whenever a reference to it is made in the text.

We shall next give simplified descriptions of the architectural components and also give an overview of their interaction.

1.1 CPU

The main functions of the CPU are (1) program execution and (2) handling of interruptions. A program is a sequence of instructions taken from the instruction set specified by the architecture. Instructions are executed in the sequence in which they appear in a program, except where such sequence is modified by a branch instruction, as explained in Chapter 2. An interruption causes the CPU to suspend temporarily the execution of a running program and to execute an interruption handling program. Interruptions are caused by a set of specified events (e.g., machine check or completion of an I/O operation) and the architecture specifies hardware-created codes for each event that causes an interruption. The interruption handler routines make use of the code in processing the interruption. By "processing an interruption" is meant taking appropriate steps necessary to identify the source of the interruption and to perform actions for resolution of the condition presented by the interruption (e.g., notification of a waiting program that an I/O operation started by it has been completed).

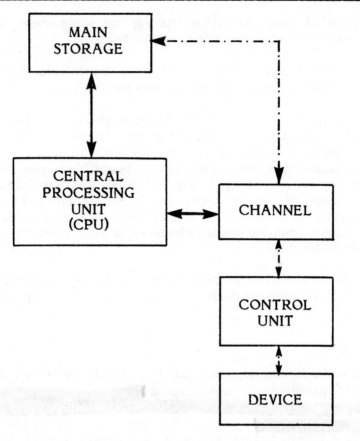

___   Path Used in Program Execution

- -   Path Used in Data Transfer from a Device

Figure 1-1/Architectural Components of
IBM Large Scale Systems

The CPU interacts with main storage and channels in the following manner:

o   **CPU/Main Storage Interaction:** CPU fetches instructions and data from main storage during program execution and modifies main storage locations if an instruction in the program specifies such modification.

o   **CPU/Channel Interaction:** CPU initiates an I/O operation by means of an I/O instruction and while the channel is performing the operation the CPU is free to execute other instructions; in other words, the CPU does not wait while the channel is performing an I/O operation. When the I/O operation is complete or has reached a pre-defined milestone, the channel interrupts the CPU (there may be several interruptions during an I/O operation).

1.2 MAIN STORAGE

The term "main storage" is used to denote physical memory that is addressable by an instruction. It is distinct from the local storage used by a CPU, comprising registers and Program Status Word (see the section on CPU Architecture for details). It is also distinct from the storage used by microcode located in the CPU, called Control Storage.

The architecture views main storage as a set of contiguous physical locations that have sequential addresses. These locations are accessed by the CPU during program execution and also by the channel when it performs an I/O operation.

1.3 CHANNEL

The function of a channel is to perform all control and data transfer operations that constitute an I/O operation. The channel interacts with the CPU, main storage, and control unit. Data transfer always takes the following physical path:

Main Storage◄───►Channel◄───►Control Unit◄───►Device

The CPU initiates an I/O operation by means of an I/O instruction, and the channel functions independently of the CPU from that point onwards. An I/O operation usually involves control operations (e.g., positioning the read/write head of a disk unit on a specific track) as well as data transfer operations (e.g., reading a record from a disk). The interaction between channel and control unit is discussed in detail in the chapters on channel architecture and device and control unit implementation.

The following principles of channel operation are reiterated since they are fundamental to the understanding of the 370 architecture:

1) the CPU is not directly involved in data transfer between device and main storage or in controlling a device; the channel performs such functions.

2) the CPU initiates an I/O operation by means of an I/O instruction and the channel carries out the operation; on completion of the I/O operation, the channel interrupts the CPU.

3) the channel communicates with a device via a control unit, while performing data transfer or control operations.

The physical connection between channel and control unit is called an interface (see Figure 5-2) and its functions are described in the chapter on control unit and device implementation.

1.4 CONTROL UNITS

The function of a control unit is to act as an intermediary between device and channel. Usually several devices are connected to a control unit and several control units are connected to a channel. The interactions between channel and control unit and between control unit and device vary greatly according to implementation. Examples of control units and their interactions between channels and devices are given in the chapters on control unit and device implementation.

1.5 DEVICES

By a device is meant a peripheral unit that is one of the end points of data transfer, the other end being main storage. Examples of devices are disks, card readers, terminals, printers and similar peripheral equipment which are used in data transfer. Usually several devices are connected to a control unit which, in turn, is connected to a channel.

1.6 ORGANIZATION OF THIS BOOK

The book is organized in three parts. Part I deals with the 370 architecture; Part II deals with implementation of the 370/168, 3033 and 3081 processors; and Part III deals with the implementation of control units and devices.

Because of the complex interactions between the various architectural components, references are often made in one chapter to descriptions given in later chapters and this might sometimes cause a certain amount of inconvenience to the reader. Also, simplified descriptions of functions of various components are given in the earlier chapters for the sake of ease of comprehension, and full details of operations are given in later chapters. This is especially true in the case of I/O operations and multiprocessing where simple descriptions are given initially and a complete treatment is postponed until an explanation of various related topics has been given.

2. CPU Architecture

The architecture specifies two main functions for the CPU, namely:

o   Program Execution

o   Handling of Interruptions

These functions are divided into several sub-functions and we shall discuss these in due course. The architecture specifies a local storage for use by CPU, comprising the following items:

o   General Registers

o   Control Registers

o   Floating Point Registers

o   Program Status Word (PSW)

This local storage is part of the CPU and is separate from the main storage; the items listed above can be manipulated in various ways by appropriate instructions. Detailed descriptions of the registers and PSW are given in later sections.

2.1 PROGRAM EXECUTION

A program is a sequence of instructions taken from the set of instructions specified in the architecture. The instruction formats and groupings of instructions by categories are discussed in another section. A program, in the sense that is used in this text, can be the operating system for the computer or an application program running under the operating system. In Appendix 1, we discuss certain operating system concepts that are intimately related to hardware architecture. The reader is advised to consult

Appendix 1 to obtain an understanding of the relative roles played by the application program, operating system, and hardware in program execution.

The architecture specifies two modes of program execution called basic control (BC) and extended control (EC). In the BC mode, a program is viewed as occupying areas of contiguous locations in main storage and the CPU executes instructions sequentially until it encounters a branch instruction which can start a new sequence. Figure 2-1 illustrates this view of program execution. The Program Status Word (PSW) has a field containing the real address of the next instruction. In the case of sequential instructions, this field is automatically incremented with the length (in bytes) of the current instruction; in the case of a branch, the branched-to address is placed in the PSW.

In the EC mode, which is the commonly used mode for the 370, a program has the option to work with real or virtual addresses (by setting bit 5 of the PSW). Under the virtual address option, a program is viewed as occupying areas of contiguous locations in virtual storage and the CPU executes instructions sequentially until it encounters a branch instruction, when a new sequence is started from the branched-to address. Figure 2-2 illustrates program execution using virtual addresses. Note that the PSW contains the virtual address of the next instruction to be executed.

The virtual addresses have to be converted to real addresses during program execution, and the architecture describes the following hardware units (called facilities) used in virtual to real address translation:

o   Dynamic Address Translation (DAT)

o   Translation Look-aside Buffer (TLB)

The functions of DAT and TLB are explained in detail in the section on virtual storage in Chapter 3. At this stage we shall only point out that the TLB stores previously translated virtual page addresses, and the DAT facility is

	MAIN STORAGE
	ADDRESS OF NEXT INSTRUCTION

PROGRAM STATUS WORD (PSW)

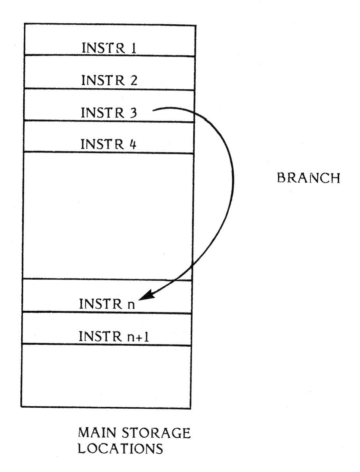

BRANCH

MAIN STORAGE
LOCATIONS

Figure 2-1/Program Layout with Real Addresses (BC Mode)

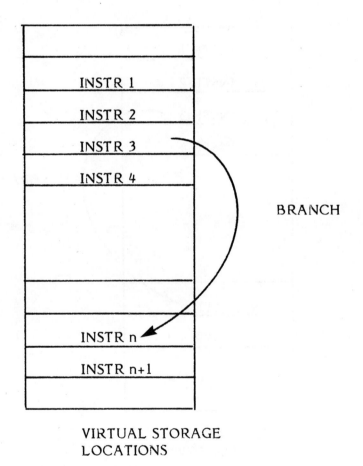

VIRTUAL STORAGE
ADDRESS OF
NEXT INSTRUCTION

PROGRAM STATUS WORD (PSW)

INSTR 1

INSTR 2

INSTR 3

INSTR 4

BRANCH

INSTR n

INSTR n+1

VIRTUAL STORAGE
LOCATIONS

Figure 2-2/Program Layout with Virtual Addresses
(EC Mode)

invoked only if the TLB does not have an entry for the virtual page.

The sub-functions performed by the CPU within the main function of program execution are the following:

o   Fetching instructions from main storage

o   Decoding instructions

o   Fetching operands from main storage

o   Translation from virtual to real addresses

o   Writing to main storage as part of program execution

o   Reading and writing from the CPU's local storage (registers and PSW).

The architecture does not specify details as to how instructions are to be fetched, decoded and executed. In the chapter on implementation we show how these operations are performed in the case of large scale processors. The architecture only requires that instructions be executed in sequence and leaves the order of fetching and decoding to the implementation.

2.2 HANDLING OF INTERRUPTIONS

An interruption is the notification of the CPU of the occurrence of a specified event or condition. The architecture groups the events and conditions that cause interruptions into six classes. Examples of events or conditions that cause interruptions are the completion of an I/O operation, a hardware error, the expiration of an interval which has been set for a timer, and an overflow in floating point arithmetical operations.

The interruption structure specified by the 370 architecture is described in detail in a later chapter. For the time being, we shall note the following characteristics of interruptions:

1) a program that is running on the CPU can disallow
    certain classes of interruptions, and in such a case, the
    CPU is said to be disabled for those classes of inter-
    ruptions (the CPU is said to be enabled when it is not
    disabled);

2) when the CPU is enabled for interruption, an executing
    program is suspended by the hardware when an inter-
    ruption occurs and a new program for handling the
    interrupt is initiated by switching PSWs.

2.3 REGISTERS AND PSW

The CPU uses information contained in its local storage
for program execution. This local storage is not part of
the main storage and contains general registers, floating
point registers, control registers, and the program status
word (PSW).

General Registers. There are sixteen 32-bit general
registers, numbered from 0 to 15. The general registers are used in arithmetic and logical operations as
well as in address generation. The instruction formats
applicable to general registers and the use of these
registers in address generation is described in the
section on instruction formats.

Control Registers. There are sixteen 32-bit control
registers, numbered from 0 to 15. Unlike general
registers, they are not available for use by application
programs. The control registers are used for performing specific system functions and storing system
parameters such as (1) addresses of segment tables
used in dynamic address translation (described in the
chapter on storage architecure) and (2) masking bits
for disabling certain types of interruptions (described
in the chapter on interruption structure).

Floating Point Registers. There are four 64-bit floating point registers which are used for floating point
arithmetical operations.

Program Status Word (PSW). The program status word is 64 bits in length, and it has two different formats depending on whether the basic control (BC) mode or extended control mode (EC) is used. The BC mode is used for providing IBM 360 PSW format compatibility and does not support virtual storage operations. The EC mode, on the other hand, is an integral part of the 370 architecture and we shall be discussing only the EC mode in the rest of this book. Figure 2-3 shows the format of the PSW in the EC mode. The PSW contains the following types of information:

o   Mask bits

o   PSW key

o   CPU states

o   Condition code

o   Address of the next instruction

ᵣefore we describe the contents of the various PSW fields, it is important to understand the role of the PSW in program execution and interruption handling.

Role of the PSW in program execution. The PSW always contains the address of the next instruction to be executed, and when the virtual address option (bit 5 turned on) is used, the address represented by bits 40 through 63 of the PSW is the virtual address of the next instruction. In the case of sequential instruction execution, the PSW updates its instruction address field by adding the instruction length to the current contents of the field. For example, if I is the virtual address of the current instruction which has a length of K bytes, then the contents of the instruction address field of the PSW is I + K. In the case of an instruction that causes a branch, a branch address replaces the instruction address field of the PSW if the branch is taken by the program; if the branch is not

	M		T	M	M	KEY	E	M		W	P		C	C	M	M	M	M				I	

0 1   5   6   7 8-11   12 13 14 15   18 19 20   23   40   63

Explanation

The Program Status Word (PSW) has 64 bits which contain the following control information:

- Masking of Interruptions, indicated by M

- Translation Invocation, indicated by T

- Storage Access Key, indicated by KEY

- Extended Control (EC) Mode, indicated by E

- CPU in wait state, indicated by W

- CPU in problem state, indicated by P

- Condition Code set by certain instructions, indicated by C

- Address of the next instruction (24 bits), indicated by I

Figure 2-3/Program Status Word (PSW) in the EC Mode

taken, normal sequential instruction execution is performed and the PSW contains the address of the next instruction.

Role of the PSW in Interruption. Interruptions are discussed in detail in another chapter, and at this point we shall describe only the role of the PSW in interruptions. An interruption suspends temporarily the currently executing program and the CPU starts executing a new program designed to process the interruption (usually called an interruption handler). The 370 architecture requires the CPU to perform the following PSW-related functions when an interruption is received by the CPU (assuming that the CPU is enabled to accept the interruption):

1)   Save the current PSW by storing its contents in a pre-assigned main storage location.

2)   Load the PSW with the contents of a pre-assigned main storage location.

An interruption handler is an operating systems routine that is executed after step (2) and this routine usually saves general registers pertaining to the old program (see Appendix 1). The status of an interrupted program is saved by storing the PSW and general registers.

We shall next discuss the various fields contained in the PSW.

o   Masking Bits: The function of these bits is to disable interruptions from certain sources. For instance, if bit 6 is off, the CPU is disabled for all I/O interruptions; when bit 6 is on, interruptions from those channels whose corresponding masking bits in Control Register 2 are on can take place.

o   PSW Key: The PSW key is used in conjunction with storage protection. Main storage, under the 370 architecture, is protected from unauthorized use and for a storage access to be successful the PSW key should match against a storage key. Details are given in the chapter on storage architecture.

o   CPU States: Two bits in the PSW indicate the states of the CPU: wait/running and problem/supervisory. The reader is referred to the section on states of the CPU for details.

o   Condition Code: Two bits indicate the condition resulting from arithmetic and logical and I/O operations. Examples of conditions are the following:

> o   a Start I/O has been successful.

> o   the sum of two numbers is less than zero.

> o   a comparison shows that two operands are equal.

A branch on condition instruction can be used to test the condition code and to branch to the appropriate instruction address.

o   Instruction Address: As mentioned before, the PSW contains a 24-bit address field that designates the virtual address of the next instruction.

2.4 STATES OF THE CPU

The architecture of the 370 specifies several states for the processor, with a three level hierarchy (see Figures 2-4 and 2-5). In the first level of the hierarchy, the processor is assigned one of the following states:

o   Stopped

o   Operating

o   Load

o   Check-Stop

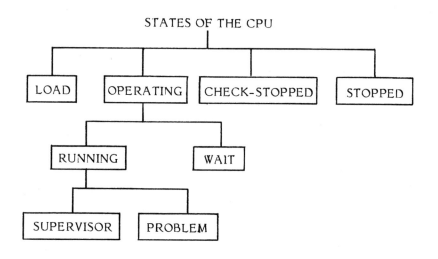

Figure 2-4/ Hierarchy of CPU States

Of these four states, the operating state represents the normal operation of the computer, namely program execution and interruption handling.

The stopped state is entered when an operator presses the STOP key on the console or, in the case of tightly-coupled multiprocessing, when one CPU signals the other CPU to enter the stopped state. When the CPU is in the stopped state, it can process only the restart interruption. By pressing the START or RESTART key, the transition from stopped to operating state can be effected.

The CPU enters the load state during initial program loading (IPL), which is activated via the LOAD NORMAL or LOAD CLEAR key. At the end of successful IPL operation, the CPU can enter the operating or stopped state, and in the case of unsuccessful IPL, it remains in the load state. The IPL operation is discussed in Appendix 1.

The check-stop state is entered from the operating state as a result of hardware malfunction and the CPU does not accept instructions or interruptions.

The operating state, as mentioned earlier, is the state wherein the processor functions in its normal role, by executing application or system programs and servicing interruptions. There are sub-levels in the hierarchy of states at the operating state level, and depending on bit settings of the PSW under program control, the processor can be in a wait or running state; if it is in a running state, it can be in a problem or supervisor state.

The processor is in a wait state if bit 14 of the PSW is set to one. Usually it is put in the wait state by the operating system dispatcher when the queue of tasks or other dispatchable entities is empty, meaning there is no work to be performed by the CPU (see Appendix 1). This can happen because application or system programs that are being executed are waiting for the completion of I/O operations, and as soon as an interruption occurs, the CPU is put back into the running state. In the wait state there is no instruction execution, but an interruption is processed

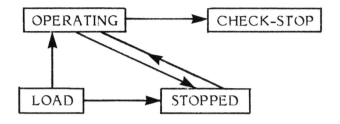

(a) STATES OF THE PROCESSOR

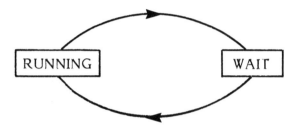

(b) SUB-STATES WITHIN OPERATING STATE

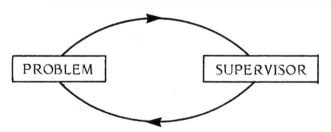

(c) SUB-STATES WITHIN RUNNING SUB-STATE

TRANSITION BETWEEN STATES

Figure 2-5/Transition Between States

in the usual manner and the processor changes its state from wait to running after an interruption.

When the processor is in the running state, it can be either in the problem state or supervisor state (bit 15 of the PSW is set to one or zero). In the problem state the processor executes only a subset of its instructions, but in the supervisor state it can execute all instructions. The distinction between the two states comes about because of the restrictions placed on application programs by the operating system. Application programs are allowed to perform logical and arithmetic operations pertaining to their problem solving functions but are restricted by the operating system from undertaking activities that can be classified as global or system-wide. For instance, no application program can directly issue an I/O instruction (e.g., Start I/O) or a control instruction (e.g., Load PSW, Load Control Registers, Store Control Registers, Set Clock, etc.). Control instructions and I/O instructions are called privileged instructions and can be executed only when the processor is in the supervisor state. The application program cannot perform certain functions which are the prerogative of the operating system, namely storage management, task management, and interruption handling, to name a few. In such a case the application program issues a supervisor call (SVC) which causes an interruption and the passing of control to the operating system, which performs the required functions in a supervisor state. SVC calls are discussed in the section on interruptions and also in Appendix 1. To sum up, the distinction between problem state and supervisor state corresponds to the division of work between application programs and the operating system; an SVC call by an application program is a means of transition between problem and supervisor states.

2.5 INSTRUCTION SET

The instruction repertoire used by the CPU can be divided into the following classes:

o   System Control Instructions

o   Arithmetic and Logical Instructions

o   Input/Output Instructions

The System Control Instructions are privileged instructions that are used by the operating system to perform storage key insertions, program status word load, control register load and similar functions. The arithmetic instructions are subdivided into binary fixed point, binary floating point and decimal instructions. The logical instructions comprise shifting, branching, comparing, and moving operations. The I/O instructions are Start I/O, Start I/O Fast Release, Halt I/O, Halt Device, Test Channel, Test I/O, Store Channel ID, Clear Channel, and Clear I/O, which are discussed in the chapter on channel architecture.

Instruction Formats. The architecture specifies eight instruction formats and every instruction has to be in one of these formats. The instruction lengths are multiples of two bytes and an instruction can be two, four or six bytes long. Figure 2-6 shows the allowable instruction formats. An explanation of the symbols used in Figure 2-6 is given below.

The instruction formats use the following symbols for registers, displacements, lengths, and binary values (also called "immediate" values).

Registers -- R, X, B

Displacement -- D

Immediate Value -- I

Length -- L

With the exception of the RS format which may use three operands, all other formats use two operands. A subscript indicates whether the entity is a first oper- and or a second operand. For instance, in the RS format R_1 is the first operand, (B_2, D_2) denote the second operand and R_3 denotes the third operand.

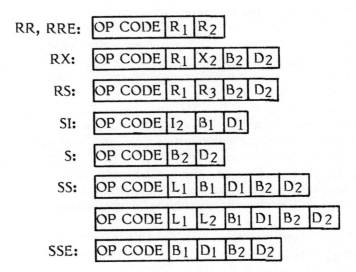

Figure 2-6/370 Instruction Formats

R_i Operands. The symbol R_1 indicates that the first operand is defined as the contents of the register whose value is specified as R_1. The symbol R_2 indicates that the second operand is defined as the contents of the register whose value is specified as R_2.

In the case of R_3, the value of R_3 may denote a register whose contents are the third operand or may denote a mask, depending on the instruction.

B_i, D_i, X_i Operands: The sets of operands represented by (B_1, D_1), (B_2, D_2), (X_2, B_2, D_2) indicate the storage address in main storage of the first or second operand as indicated by the suffix. We shall use the notation specified in the architecture in describing the use of these symbols. The set (B_1, D_1) and (B_2, D_2) are denoted as $D_1(B_1)$, $D_2(B_2)$; (X_2, B_2, D_2) is denoted as $D_2(X_2, B_2)$.

B_i, $i=1, 2$ is a register called the base register. D_i, $i=1,2$ is a 12-bit binary number called the displacement. X_i, $i=2$ is a register called the index register.

$D_2(X_2, B_2)$ is short-hand notation for indicating that the address of the second operand is obtained by adding the contents of registers specified by X_2 and B_2 to D_2. For example, if the contents of registers 2 and 1 are 4000 and 5000, respectively, then 1000 (1,2) is equivalent to $1000 + 4000 + 5000 = 10,000$.

Likewise, $D_1(B_1)$ and $D_2(B_2)$ indicate that the address of the first or second operand is obtained by adding D_1 to the contents of B_1 or D_2 to the contents of B_2. Thus, 1000 (2) is equivalent to $1000 + 4000 = 5000$.

I_2 Operand: The I_2 operand is one byte in length and contains a binary number which is used as the second operand in performing the specified operation.

L_i Operand: L_1 and L_2 specify lengths of data specified by $D_1(B_1)$ and $D_2(B_2)$. The architecture uses the notation $D_i(L_i, B_i)$ to indicate that the operand address starts at location D_i (B_i) and the length of the operand is L_i plus one. The specification of length is necessary in many situations; for example, if decimal multiplication between the operands is desired, it is necessary to specify the location as well as the length of both operands.

We shall briefly describe next the various instruction formats specified by the architecture, namely:

o   Register and register operation (RR, RRE)

o   Register and indexed storage operation (RX)

o   Register and storage operation (RS)

o   Storage and immediate operation (SI)

o   Storage and implied operand operation (S)

o   Storage and storage operation (SS, SSE)

<u>Register and Register Operation.</u>   The RR and RRE formats use contents of registers for both operands. Examples of RR operations are the following:

o   Arithmetical operations (addition, subtraction, multiplication, division)

o   Logical operations (and, or)

o   Comparison

o   Branching

o   Move character strings

The last operation involves moving data items from one storage location to another, but its format is RR and the address of pertinent locations are given in the registers.   RRE operations are register operations using an extended (i.e., larger) operation code field.

Register and Indexed Storage Operation. The RX format uses the contents of the register whose value is given by R_1 as the first operand and $D_2(X_2, B_2)$ as the address of the second operand. By incrementing X_2, a program can step through arrays without modifying D_2 or B_2, and in situations involving a program loop, only the contents of X_2 need be modified. Examples of RX operations are the following:

o Arithmetic operations (addition, subtraction, multiplication, division)
o Logical operations (and, or)
o Comparison
o Branching

The process of modification of the value of X_2 is generally known by the name of indexing.

Register and Storage Operation. The RS format specifies contents of R_1 as its first operand and $D_2(B_2)$ as the address of the second operand. The following is a list of important RS instructions:

o Storing the contents of a set of registers
o Loading a set of registers
o Branching
o Shifting

The use of the R_3 field depends on the instruction.

Storage Immediate Operations. The first operand address is given by $D_1(B_1)$; the second operand is the binary value specified by I_2. The instructions in this group are primarily logical and control instructions.

Storage and Implied Operand Operations. The instructions within this category use the S format. The second operand address is given by $D_2(B_2)$ and the first operand is implied. I/O instructions as well as several control instructions (Insert PSW, Store PSW, etc.) use the S format and in some cases the B_2 and D_2 fields are used in special ways that are dependent on the instruction.

Storage and Storage Operations. The SS and SSE formats use two addresses for two operands. The SSE format uses an extended operation code field and is rarely encountered, except for certain control instructions (e.g., testing an address for storage protection) and we shall not discuss it any further.

The SS instructions are used for the following operations:

o   Decimal arithmetic operations (addition, subtraction, multiplication, division)
o   Logical operations
o   Comparison operations
o   Data manipulation operations
o   Translation (e.g., from one data code to another)

The operands have their lengths specified by L_1 and L_2.

Instruction Features and Instruction Sets. Instructions are grouped into features, on the basis of functions performed by them. Examples of these features are listed below:

o   Floating Point
o   Extended Precision Floating Point
o   Multiprocessing
o   Recovery Extensions

Instructions are also grouped into sets and the architecture specifies the following:

o   Commercial Instruction Set
o   Standard Instruction Set
o   Universal Instruction Set

Every CPU having the 370 architecture is expected to execute the Commercial Instruction Set, which consists of fixed point and decimal arithmetic instructions, logical instructions, I/O instructions, and control instructions.

The Standard Instruction Set consists of the Commercial Instruction Set without decimal instructions. The Universal Instruction Set consists of the Commercial

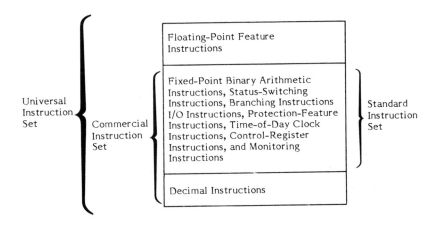

Figure 2-7/Classification of the 370 Instruction Set

Instruction Set and the Floating Point Feature (see Figure 2-7).

Instruction Execution. An instruction is usually indivisibly executed and interruptions take place at the end of the instruction; the only exceptions are two instructions which move long data strings and these can be interrupted at various stages of execution.

A unit of operation is either an entire instruction or a part of an instruction that is indivisibly executed before an interruption is allowed.

An instruction need not always be successfully executed. The architecture specifies the following possibilities for the ending of non-interruptible instructions:

1. Completion -- the instruction is successfully executed and the PSW contains the address of the next instruction.
2. Suppression -- the fields in the PSW that are normally modified by an instruction are left unchanged and the address field in the PSW contains the address of the next sequential instruction.
3. Nullification -- the result of nullification is the same as that of suppression except that when an interruption follows nullification, the address in the PSW is that of the nullified instruction.
4. Termination -- the result of termination or PSW fields is unpredictable.

In the case of interruptible instructions, the architecture specifies a set of detailed rules for each type of ending but we shall not describe those here.

2.6 COMMENTS

We have attempted to give only an overview of the CPU architecture and for a detailed treatment on instruction sets, states of the CPU and related topics the reader is referred to the "IBM System/370 Principles of Operation Manual."

3. Storage Architecture

The 370 architecture specifies three types of storage, namely:

o   Main Storage

o   Real Storage

o   Virtual Storage

The distinction between real storage and main storage is valid only in tightly-coupled multiprocessing systems; in the case of systems having only a single CPU, main storage and real storage can be used synonymously. Main storage is physically realized in terms of semiconductor memory in the case of present day large-scale computers. Virtual storage, on the other hand, is a conceptual entity and exists only as a set of addresses which have physical representation only when translated.

3.1 MAIN STORAGE

Main storage is a physical collection of bytes that have sequential addresses (called absolute addresses) starting from zero. The basic addressable unit is a byte and the absolute address of a byte is used in all main storage addresses. An absolute address is necessary for reading from or writing to main storage by the two users of main storage, namely the CPU and channel(s).

Half Words, Full Words, and Double Words. As mentioned earlier, a byte is the smallest addressable unit in main storage. Assume that the bytes are numbered 0,1,2,3,4,5,6,7,8,9,10,11 ... Then the groups of bytes (0,1), (2,3), (4,5), (6,7), (8,9), (10,11) ... are called half-words. A half-word is a collection of two bytes located on a two-byte boundary; that is, the address of the first byte must be a multiple of 2. A full word is a group of four bytes such that the address of the first byte is a multiple of 4.   Thus, (0,1,2,3), (4,5,6,7), (8,9,10,11) are full words. Finally, a double word is a group of eight bytes such that the address of the first byte is a multiple of 8 as exemplified by (0,1,2,3,4,5, 6,7), (8,9,10,11,12,13,14,15) and so on.   A half-word, full word and double word start on two-, four- and eight-byte boundaries.

Data Representation. The binary string of 8-bit data contained in a byte is often viewed as representing a character.   For instance, characters read from a punched card are internally represented in main storage by the bit patterns in a byte. The 370 architecture uses a code known as Extended Binary-Coded-Decimal Interchange Code (EBCDIC), which provides binary representations for characters used in data transmission.

3.2 REAL STORAGE

Real storage is synonymous with main storage when there is no multiprocessing, i.e., when only one CPU uses main storage.   As mentioned earlier, in such a case the CPU uses an absolute address for accessing a main storage location. In the case of multiprocessing, each CPU uses a "real" address to access a main storage location; this "real" address is converted into an absolute address by a mechanism known as prefixing.

Each CPU needs the first 4K byte locations of main storage for storing PSWs and other data that is essential for its functioning. When there is only one CPU in the system, the first 4K main storage locations starting from zero are assigned to the CPU for this purpose. Under multiprocessing, each CPU is given 4K locations for its own use but the starting address of these locations is no longer zero. A CPU can function only by assuming that 0 to 4K-1 bytes of main storage are available to it for housekeeping functions and this conflict is resolved by means of prefixing, whereby the CPU address (called the real address) is mapped to an absolute main storage address by a hardware device.

Prefixing is explained in the chapter on multiprocessing.

To summarize, real addresses are used by a CPU in a multiprocessing environment, on the assumption that the first 4K locations of main storage is available to it for housekeeping purposes; the real address is then mapped to an absolute storage location by means of prefixing. Real storage is main storage re-numbered in real address sequence.

3.3 VIRTUAL STORAGE

We saw in previous sections that the 370 architecture provided for a 24-bit storage address whose address formation rules can be summarized as follows:

1) In executing instructions, the base address, index, and displacement are added to obtain a 24-bit binary integer;

2) Bits 40 through 63 of the PSW contain a 24-bit address of the next instruction to be executed.

The 24 bit address field in the PSW provides for an address range of 16,777,216 bytes which is equal to 16 mega bytes (MB). The real storage available for most IBM computers (with the exception of the 3033 and 3081) is only a fraction of this allowable address range. For example, the 370/168 can have a maximum of 8 MB of real storage.

Virtual storage offers the capability of utilizing the maximum addressing range provided by the 24 address bits. Virtual storage locations can be thought of as cells numbered from 0 to 16 MB minus one and programs use these numbers (called virtual addresses) instead of main storage addresses. The motivations for virtual storage arose out of difficulties encountered in early multi-programming systems in which each application program used real storage addressing. This caused certain problems in the efficient utilization of main storage as well as in the writing of application programs. Because they used real addresses, programs had often to be loaded in the same area of real storage. Furthermore, a program often had to wait for loading until a contiguous area of storage locations which would fit its size was available. This resulted in storage fragmentation, meaning that there were "holes" or unused areas in real storage. Also, it was the responsibility of the application programmer to conserve real storage by over-laying program modules.

Virtual storage architecture provides an elegant solution to the above mentioned difficulties by requiring that pro-grams use virtual addresses instead of real addresses and using a page as a basis of storage allocation. Thus, during the concurrent execution of multiple programs, real stor-age contains pages belonging to several programs; real storage is allocated to the programs on a demand basis and taken away from them on a basis of utilization.

Listed below are the central concepts used in virtual storage architecture:

1) Programs do not use real addresses but virtual addres-ses, which are converted to real addresses using dyna-mic address translation (DAT);

2) Virtual storage is organized into address spaces, seg-ments, pages, and bytes;

3) A page of virtual storage resides physically in main storage or auxiliary storage (e.g., drum or disk).

Virtual Storage Organization. Virtual storage is organ-ized hierarchically into address space, segment, page and byte as illustrated in Figure 3-1. An address space is the maximum virtual storage available to a program (i.e., 16 MB under the 24-bit addressing scheme). There may be multiple address spaces in a multipro-gramming environment and each address space is given a unique ID. An address space can be represented by a set of sequential integers (corresponding to byte addresses) ranging from zero to the maximum virtual storage size of 16 MB minus one. Within an address

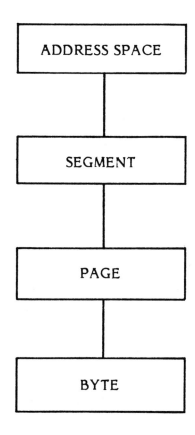

Figure 3-1/ Organization of Virtual Storage

space, virtual storage is divided into segments. A segment is a block of contiguous virtual storage and its size can be either 64 KB or 1 MB. A page is a block of contiguous virtual storage within a segment and its size can be either 2 KB or 4 KB. Figure 3-2 shows the division of an address space into segments and pages.

Virtual Storage Addressing. A virtual address comprises a segment index, page index, and byte index as shown in Figure 3-3. The idea is to uniquely identify a byte within an address space by specifying a segment number, a page number, and a byte number. As mentioned before, an address space can be divided into 256 segments and each segment can be divided into 16 pages (using 64 KB and 4 KB for segment and page sizes). In such a case, the segment index can assume values from 0 to 255, the page index can assume values from 0 to 15, and the byte index varies from 0 to 4K minus one.

Multiple Address Spaces. An address space can contain several programs, each occupying a set of contiguous virtual storage locations. It is the role of the operating system to assign virtual addresses to programs (see Appendix 1). Some operating systems (e.g., Single Virtual Storage (SVS) operating system) use only one address space and assign virtual locations to programs within that address space. Other operating systems (e.g., Multiple Virtual Storage (MVS) operating system) allow multiple address spaces and each address space can contain one or more programs, as shown in Figure 3-4.

At this stage, we shall present only certain intuitive ideas which will aid in understanding how programs are run under virtual storage architecture. First of all, the 16 MB virtual storage available under the 24-bit architecture can be viewed as a single entity and programs can be assigned locations within this virtual storage, as is done under the SVS operating system.

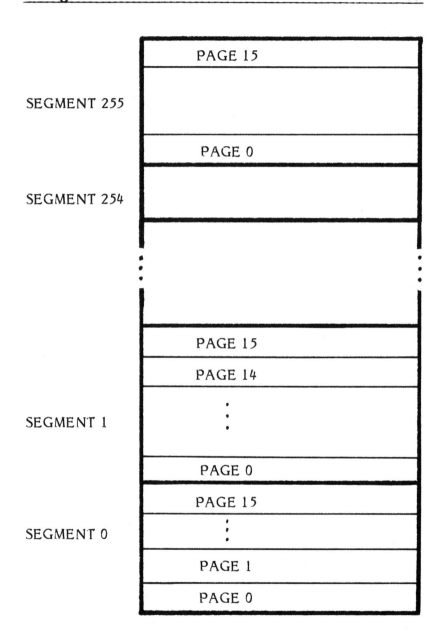

Figure 3-2/16 MB Address Space Divided Into
64 KB Segments and 4 KB Pages

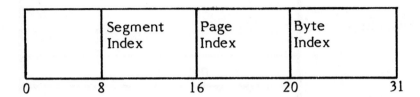

Figure 3-3/24-Bit Virtual Address Format for
64 K Segments and 4 K-Byte Pages

Secondly, an extra tag, called the address space ID, can be introduced in the hardware and software, and a virtual storage of 16 MB can be assigned to several such tags, as is done under MVS. Each 16 MB virtual storage assignment then becomes an address space, and the operating system assigns blocks of addresses within that address space to various programs and data areas.

Virtual Storage Operations. A page in virtual storage is temporarily mapped into a page frame in main storage or a page slot in auxiliary storage during program execution. In other words, a page is a conceptual entity that is given physical realization by a set of contiguous locations (having the same size as the page) in either main storage or auxiliary storage. Figure 3-5 shows how a 4K page is mapped to a 4K page frame and a 4K page slot. Figure 3-6 shows three commonly encountered page operations. The transfer of a slot to a frame is called a page-in; the transfer of a frame to a slot is called a page-out. A page-fix is a long-term assignment of a page to a page-frame.

3.4 DYNAMIC ADDRESS TRANSLATION

As seen from the previous section, virtual storage architecture provides a set of rules for using addresses within programs that is independent of main storage considerations. During program execution, however, instructions and operands have to be fetched from main storage. The instruction and operand addresses are virtual and they have to be converted to real addresses before execution of an instruction can take place. In the case of tightly coupled multiprocessing systems, the real address is further converted to an absolute main storage address by means of prefixing, as described in the section on multiprocessing; for a single CPU, main storage and real storage can be used interchangeably. In summary, the following rules must be observed during program execution:

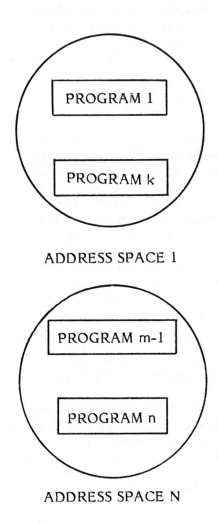

ADDRESS SPACE 1

ADDRESS SPACE N

Figure 3-4/Programs and Address Spaces

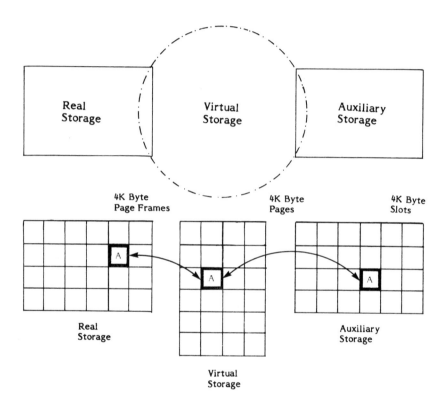

Figure 3-5/Mapping of a Page

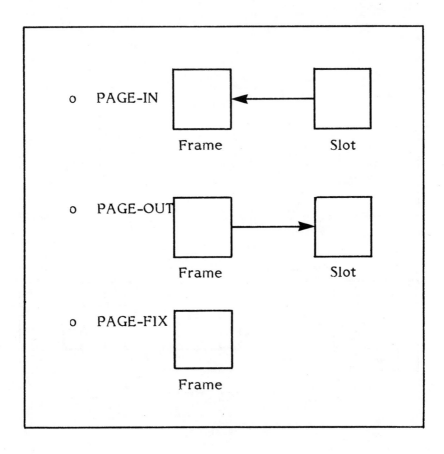

Figure 3-6/Page Operations

1) A virtual page has to be assigned a page frame in real storage;

2) A virtual address is converted to a real storage address;

3) A real storage address is converted to an absolute main storage address in the case of tightly-coupled multiprocessing systems.

The process of conversion of virtual addresses of instructions and instruction operands in an address space into real storage addresses is known as dynamic address translation (DAT).

The translation is done by hardware which references the following:

o   Control Registers 0 and 1

o   Segment Tables (in real storage)

o   Page Tables (in real storage)

The architecture provides for page sizes of 2K and 4K, and segment sizes of 64K and 1M. (A page size of 4K and a segment size of 64K is used by the MVS Operating System.) The page and segment sizes are input parameters of the translation procedure and are contained in Control Register 0.

The translation procedure is schematically illustrated in Figure 3-7, and in the following discussion it is assumed that 4K pages and 64K segments are used. (In the case of other page or segment sizes, a similar procedure is applicable.) The virtual address consists of a segment index, page index, and byte index. The translation procedure converts a virtual page represented by the segment index and page index to a page frame address in real storage. The byte index is not converted but added to the page frame address.

There is a segment table for every 16 MB virtual address space. The table has 256 entries (one per segment), and each entry contains the address of a page table, a bit (F1) for segment validity, and the length of the page table (see Figure 3-7). The page table contains 16 entries for the segment (one per page), and each entry contains the address of a page frame and one flag bit.

The segment table and page tables associated with all active address spaces are always kept in real storage. These tables are created by the operating system at the time of initializing an address space. The page table entries change during the course of program execution because a page may be moved out of a page frame in real storage to a slot in auxiliary storage to make room for another page from the same or different address space. The MVS operating system, for instance, has page replacement algorithms which are designed to optimally allocate page frames among contending address spaces (see Appendix 1). The flag bit (F2) in the page table entry indicates whether the page frame address is valid or invalid. This bit is set to zero by the operating system to indicate that the page has a page frame assigned to it, as shown by the page table entry. The bit is set to one by the operating system when the page frame is taken away from the page and allocated to another, or when the page is not assigned a frame.

The address of the segment table is contained in Control Register 1, and the operating system loads the register with this information when it decides to execute programs in an address space.

The virtual to real address translation procedure (see Figure 3-7) works as follows:

1) The segment index K is multiplied by 4 (the segment table entry size is 4 bytes) and added to the segment table address given in Control Register 1, to obtain an offset to the Kth entry in the segment table.

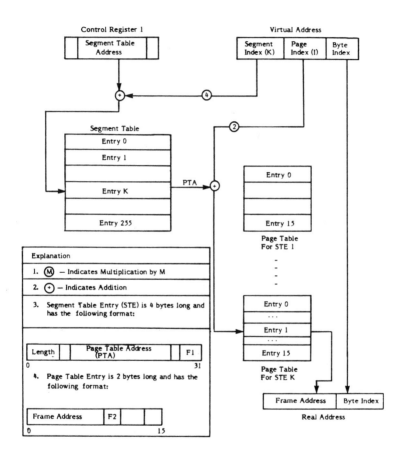

Figure 3-7/Dynamic Address Translation Procedure

2) The page table address (PTA) from the segment table entry is added to the page index (I) times 2 (the page table entry size is 2 bytes) to obtain an offset to the page table entry; it is assumed that the flag bit F1 shows that the segment is valid and, if it is not, a program interruption (segment translation exception) occurs.

3) The offset to the page table entry obtained in the above step is used in examining the entry in the page table; if the F2 bit shows that the entry is valid, the address of the page frame is concatenated with the byte index to obtain the real address; if the entry is not valid, a program interruption (page translation exception) occurs.

A numerical example of dynamic address translation is shown in Figure 3-8. The segment index 2 is used to obtain the second entry in the segment table. The page table location for the second segment is 20,000 and the third entry of the page table (corresponding to page index 3) is used to obtain the address of the page frame (shown as 208,100) occupied by the virtual page. The byte index of 104 is added to this address to obtain a real address of 208,104.

Translation-Lookaside Buffer. The function of the translation-lookaside buffer (TLB) is to store translated real addresses of page frames to minimize the frequency of dynamic address translation. In the previous section we saw that the byte index of the virtual address was the same as the byte index of the real address (see Figure 3-7) and that the translation procedure essentially consisted of obtaining a page frame address corresponding to the segment and page indexes. This means that if the instructions in a virtual 4K page are executed in sequence, the same page address can be used for all instructions within the page. The TLB is designed to store previously translated page frame addresses and the corresponding

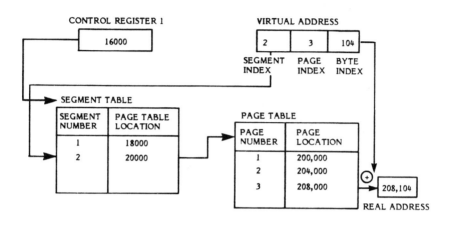

Figure 3-8/Numerical Example for Dynamic
Address Translation

segment and page indexes.   A detailed example of the structure of the TLB is given in the section on the 3033 implementation.

3.5   STORAGE PROTECTION AND REFERENCE AND CHANGE INDICATORS

The 370 architecture specifies keys to be used in connection with storage protection, storage reference, and storage update.   ¬efore discussing details of these specifications, we shall present certain underlying concepts.

Storage protection is necessary because multiple address spaces execute concurrently under an operating system like MVS, and the real storage used by one address space is protected against violation by another address space.   The operating system itself needs protection of real storage areas that it uses for maintaining tables, queues, and other data areas as well as the critical part of its code, called the nucleus, which also is kept in real storage.

The operating system also has to know whether or not a page frame has been used during given periods of time by any one of the concurrently executing address spaces so that it can reallocate pages according to usage among competing address spaces.   This usage can be of two kinds, namely, reference or change.   When a byte within a page frame is read by the CPU or a channel, a reference indicator is set by hardware; likewise, when a byte within a page frame is modified by the CPU or a channel, a change indicator is set by hardware.

Storage Protection Key.   Main storage is organized into 2K blocks, and for every block there is a 7-bit key having four fields, as described in Figure 3-9.   ¬its 0 through 3 contain the protection key for a specific 2K storage block.   For every request for a main storage operation involving that block, a matching key should be present in the Program Status Word (PSW) or Channel Status Word (CSW).

The architecture does not specify where the keys are

to be stored; for a specific implementation, the reader is referred to the section on 3033 implementation.

The Fetch Protection Bit is used in the following manner: a zero implies that protection is applicable only to storing data in main storage and not to fetching; a one implies that both storing and fetching are protected.

The Reference Bit is set to one when a main storage location in the corresponding block is referenced either for fetching or storing.

The Change Bit is set to one when a main storage location in the corresponding block is updated by a storage operation.

The Reference and Change Bits are used by the MVS operating system in real storage management. The operating system, in order to manage real storage efficiently, has to know the following information pertaining to page frames:

o   the period for which a page frame has gone unreferenced.

o   whether or not the contents of a page frame have been modified as a result of either program activity or channel activity.

This enables the operating system to reassign page frames among multiple programs and also to page-out the modified page frames before they are reassigned.

We shall list here the various aspects of storage protection:

1)   The CPU uses a key contained in the PSW and the channel uses a key contained in the Channel Status Word for accessing main storage.

For protection purposes, storage is organized into 2K Byte Blocks; each Block has a key, having the following format:

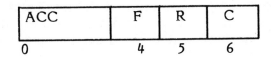

o   ACC = Access Key is matched with key in PSW, or key in the Channel Address Word (CAW), to validate storage access.

o   F = 0 Indicates Store Protection.

o   F = 1 Indicates both Store and Fetch Protection.

o   R = 1 Indicates that the 2K Block has been referenced by CPU or Channel.

o   R = 0 Indicates that the 2K Block has not been referenced.

o   C - 1 Indicates that the 2K Block has been updated by CPU or Channel.

o   C - 0 Indicates that the 2K Block has not been updated by CPU or Channel.

Figure 3-9/Storage Protection

2) The key for each 2K block of main storage is matched against the access key used by CPU or channel. If the keys do not match, the storage operation does not take place and a program interruption denoting storage protection violation is generated by the hardware if the CPU is requesting the operation; a protection check is indicated in the Channel Status Word (CSW) if the channel is requesting the operation.

3) Not all accesses to main storage by CPU or channel are subject to storage protection; examples of operations where key-controlled protection are not applicable are the following:

    o   Interruptions

    o   Dynamic address translation

    o   Updating an interval timer

4) The storage key can be read or changed by the following privileged instructions:

    o   Insert storage key loads the storage key into a specified register.

    o   Insert Reference Bit (changes ACC in Figure 3-9)

    o   Reset Reference Bit (changes R in Figure 3-9)

    o   Set Storage Key (changes ACC, F, R, C in Figure 3-9)

Low Address Protection. This feature is used to protect the contents of real storage locations 0 to 511 (which are used by the CPU in interruption handling, for example) from changing as a result of writing by unauthorized programs. Bit 3 of Control Register 0 is used for controlling low address protection: when the bit is set to one, low address protection is guaranteed; where the bit is zero there is no such guarantee.

4. Interruption Structure

In this section we shall describe the interruption structure provided by the 370 architecture. As mentioned previously, an interruption is the notification of the CPU of the occurrence of an event that has to be processed by routines, called interruption handlers, that are part of the operating system. In the remainder of this section we show the hardware specifications for handling interruptions as laid down in the 370 architecture and explain briefly, where appropriate, the software aspects of interruption handling with examples from the MVS operating system.

4.1 OVERVIEW OF INTERRUPTION HANDLING

Interruptions are grouped into six classes, namely I/O, external, program, supervisor call, machine check, and restart. The hardware stores the current PSW and fetches a new PSW for servicing the interruption (see Figure 4-1). For each class, there are two locations in real storage which correspond to the "old" and "new" PSWs. The "old" PSW location is used to store the current PSW; the contents of the "new" PSW location are loaded into PSW, and program execution is resumed by fetching the address shown in the new PSW. A sixteen bit interruption code is also placed by hardware in a real storage location to provide identification of the source of interruption within the class in the case of I/O, external, supervisor call and program interruptions. For instance, program interruption can be caused from any one of 21 sources -- fixed point overflow, page fault, or monitor event, to name just three. The source of I/O interruption may be channels 0 to 5, or channels 6 and upwards. In the case of certain interruption codes, the execution of the instruction given by the old PSW is either supressed or nullified (e.g., fixed point overflow). The two byte interruption code is stored in real storage locations as indicated in Figure 4-1.

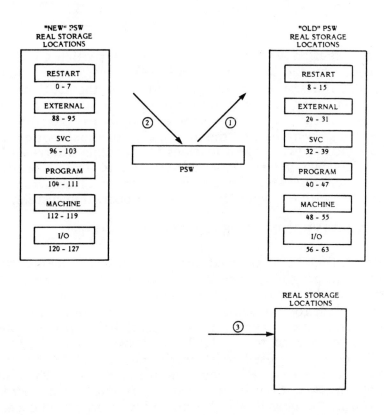

EXPLANATION: REAL STORAGE
                                LOCATIONS

1 "OLD" PSW IS SAVED

2 "NEW" PSW IS LOADED

3 INTERRUPTION CODE AND STATUS
   (WHERE APPLICABLE) IS ENTERED

Figure 4-1/Hardware Interruption Action

Additional information is provided in the case of certain interruptions. In the case of I/O interruptions the contents of the Channel Status Word (CSW) is stored in a fixed real storage location, and further information is available at fixed real storage locations. In the case of program interruptions, additional information is provided in fixed real storage locations.

We shall bring up again the distinction between real storage locations and absolute storage locations as explained in the chapter on storage architecture. When there is only one CPU accessing main storage, the real and absolute storage locations are identical. When two CPUs access the same main storage (as in the case of tightly coupled multiprocessing systems), each CPU uses the same real storage locations in performing its functions. For instance, the hardware stores the "old" PSW for supervisor call interruption in real storage locations 32 through 39 in the case of either CPU. To avoid destruction of information stored by one CPU by another CPU, each CPU is assigned a separate 4K location in main storage. The range of real addresses 0-4K minus one for each CPU is converted to its assigned 4K location by means of prefixing, which is explained in the chapter on multiprocessing.

We shall discuss next the various classes of interruptions and the specific actions performed by the hardware in each case. Figure 4-2 shows the source and time of occurrence of the interruption for each of the six classes in an abbreviated format. The important thing to note is that an interruption in each class originates from one or more sources after the occurrence of specific events.

4.2 I/O INTERRUPTION

The source of an I/O interruption is a channel, and during the course of an I/O operation a channel may interrupt the CPU several times. A detailed discussion of I/O interruption is presented in the next chapter. For the present, we shall only make the following observations:

1) An I/O interruption is the sole means of communica-

tion by a channel to a CPU;

2) The channel notifies the CPU of the progress of an I/O operation by an interruption at the completion of the operation and also (optionally) by interruptions at various stages of the I/O operation which are called program-controlled interruptions (PCIs).

3) The hardware stores the old PSW in locations 56 through 63, loads the new PSW from locations 120 through 127, and stores the following information in specified real storage locations:

   o   Channel Status (CSW) -- A double word indicating the status of channel, control unit, and device and containing other related information is stored in real storage locations 64 through 71. (The format of the CSW is given in a later section.)

   o   Channel and Device Address -- The addresses of the interrupting channel and device are stored in real storage locations 186 through 187.

   o   Logout Information -- In case of channel error, limited channel logout information is available in real storage locations 176 through 179, and the address of extended channel logout information is placed in real storage locations 172 through 175.

The software handling of an I/O interruption is done by the I/O interruption handler and the I/O supervisor. Parts of these routines are run in a disabled mode in order to avoid a second I/O interrupt from destroying the information contained in the various real storage locations.

4.3 EXTERNAL INTERRUPTION

The sources of external interruption can be grouped into four classes: clocks, timers, another CPU, and sources connected to signal lines.

CLASS	SOURCE OF INTERRUPTION	TIME OF INTERRUPTION
I/O	Channel	On Completion of channel operation, or the occurrence of certain I/O related events
External	Timers Malfunction Alert External Signal	On the occurrence of timer expiration, malfunction alert, etc.
SVC	Program	When SVC call is issued
Program Check	Program	On Overflow/Underflow, virtual address translation error, address error, etc.
Machine Check	Hardware	On hardware malfunction
Restart	Restart Key	On pressing restart key

Figure 4-2/Interruption Classes

In each of these cases, the old PSW is stored at location 24, a new PSW is loaded from location 88, and the source of the interruption is stored in locations 134 and 135 by the hardware. We shall describe briefly the characteristics of each source.

Clocks. The 370 architecture provides for a time-of-day (TOD) clock and a clock comparator. The TOD clock may be shared by more than one CPU in a multiprocessing environment but each CPU has its own clock comparator. The TOD clock's resolution varies from model to model, depending on the speed of the CPU. The power supply to the clock may or may not be dependent on that of the CPU. The TOD clock's function is to provide a standard reference time for use by programs. The TOD clock is usually set to a standard time origin, namely January 1, 1900, 0 A.M. Greenwich Mean Time (GMT). The clock is essentially a binary counter having 64 bits and a cycle of approximately 143 years.

A clock comparator can be used by a program to specify a time value that is compared against the TOD clock time. When the latter exceeds the former, an external interruption is generated by the hardware. The clock comparator is a binary counter similar to the TOD clock, and its resolution varies according to the model. The clock comparator can be used for setting time ceilings that trigger the execution of specified programs.

Timers. The 370 architecture provides for two types of timers -- a CPU timer and an interval timer. The CPU timer is a binary counter having the same format as the TOD clock. Its functions are:

1) To provide a measure of elapsed CPU time

2) To generate an interrupt at the end of a specified CPU elapsed time.

The uses of the CPU timer are to measure CPU execution intervals for accounting and other purposes and also to indicate the end of a specified time interval on the CPU.

An interval timer provides the same functions as the CPU timer, except that its resolution is coarser.

Signals from Another CPU. In a tightly coupled multiprocessing environment, signals generated by one CPU to another CPU cause the latter to be interrupted. The section on multiprocessing gives additional details on this topic.

External Signals. The architecture provides for a direct control feature which comprises an external signal facility and read-write-direct facility. The purpose of this feature is to provide data transfer capabilities independent of those provided by channels.

4.4 SUPERVISOR CALL (SVC) INTERRUPTION

A supervisor call (SVC) is a means whereby a program can invoke the services of the operating system for performing an I/O operation, obtaining virtual storage, passing control to another program, and several such functions. The SVC instruction specifies a numerical identification parameter. Only 8 bits are provided for this parameter, which means that only 256 SVC types are allowed by the architecture.

The execution of the SVC instruction causes an interruption and the hardware (1) stores the old PSW in location 32, (2) loads a new PSW from location 96, and (3) stores in locations 34 and 35 the number of the SVC mentioned before. The new PSW contains the address of the operating system routine for SVC handling. The SVC handling routine performs the functions required by the requesting program by invoking other operating system routines and after completion of such functions returns control to the program that issued the SVC or to other system routines.

4.5 PROGRAM INTERRUPTION

A program interruption is caused by an error or abnormal condition arising from the execution of an instruction in a program. It is the function of the interruption handler (whose address is in the new PSW) to determine whether the error or condition is resolvable or not and to take appropriate measures.

The hardware places the old PSW in location 40, loads the new PSW from location 104 and stores an interruption code that identifies the cause of the interruption in locations 142 and 143.

There are several events that cause a program interruption. We shall describe only the significant ones here.

Page Translation Exception. We have seen that during dynamic address translation the address of a real page frame corresponding to a virtual page is obtained from the Page Table. If the Page Table shows that there is no real page frame entry corresponding to the virtual page, a page translation exception (also known as page fault) is created by hardware which triggers a program interruption. The program interruption handler passes control to appropriate operating system modules that assign a page frame to the page and perform a page-in operation.

Addressing Exception. When a program references a storage location which is beyond the address range of the storage configured for the CPU, an addressing exception results and an interruption is generated. For instance, assume that the processor is a 3033 and the configured storage is 8 MB; if a program references a storage location beyond the available 8 MB, an addressing exception takes place.

Protection Exception. A protection exception arises when a program references a storage location that it is not allowed to address. In other words, when a program violates storage protection conventions, a program interruption results. Storage protection is explained in the chapter on storage architecture.

Overflow and Underflow Exceptions. Overflow in the case of decimal and fixed point arithmetical operations can cause a program interruption; so can exponent overflow and underflow in the case of floating point operations. Fixed point division can cause an interruption if the divisor is zero or if the quotient overflows the register.

Privileged Operation Exception. This exception occurs when a privileged instruction (e.g., Start I/O) is issued by a program in a problem state; the operation is suppressed and an interruption takes place.

4.6 MACHINE CHECK INTERRUPTION

A machine check interruption is caused by recoverable or irrecoverable failure on the part of a hardware component, which may be a channel, CPU or storage.

The interruption stores the old PSW in location 48, copies the new PSW from location 112, and stores an 8-byte code in locations 232 through 239. In certain cases, logout information is stored in specified storage locations.

The 370 architecture groups hardware errors into various classes and subclasses. A hardware error is exigent when it is non-recoverable; it is repressible when recoverable. Error detection is provided by the addition of redundant check bits (parity bits) in program data and by timeouts for I/O instruction and interruption. Certain processors (e.g., 3033) have main storage units that contain error checking and correction (ECC) hardware that detect and rectify single bit errors. (In the case of multiple bits errors, only detection capability is provided.) Also, some processors (e.g., 3033) have "instruction retry" capabilities; i.e., an instruction is re-executed if there is an error. We shall describe briefly some of the error sub-classes that are defined under the 370 architecture.

Instruction Processing Damage. This is an exigent machine check condition and indicates that the CPU must discontinue its operation. It can be due to various causes such as malfunction in dynamic address translation, an unretryable processor error, etc.

Storage Errors. Storage errors can be due to errors in storage keys or errors in main storage. Some of the storage errors are repressible (e.g., the 3033 can self-correct a single bit processor storage error by means of its error-checking and correction (ECC) capabilities). Other errors are exigent (e.g., a multiple bit error in processor storage in the 3033).

System Recovery. This subclass of errors is repressible and indicates that malfunctions have been detected and corrected (e.g., a single bit storage error mentioned above or a similar malfunction that is correctable).

Degradation. The definition of degradation is model-dependent. For instance, in the case of the 3033, an error that results in the deletion of a row in the cache memory or an error that causes a deletion of one half of the TLB is viewed as degradation, and is treated as a repressible error.

4.7 RESTART INTERRUPTION

The restart interruption occurs as a result of the manual activation of the restart key or by another CPU in a tightly coupled multiprocessing environment issuing a restart order.

The restart interruption causes the current PSW to be stored at location 8 and copies a new PSW from location 0. The new PSW contains the address of the appropriate interruption handler routine which performs necessary functions.

4.8 POINT OF INTERRUPTION

The processor is normally allowed to complete the execution of an instruction before it is interrupted, but in the case of two instructions that involve movement of long data strings (namely COMPARE LOGICAL LONG and MOVE LONG), an interruption is permitted when the instruction is in a partial stage of completion. With the exception of the two above mentioned instructions, all other instructions are non-interruptible. The term "unit of operation" is used to describe a non-interruptible quantum of work done by the processor in instruction execution. The two interruptible instructions consist of more than one unit of operation, and the processor accepts interruptions in between units of operations. All other instructions are executed as one unit of operation.

4.9 ENABLING AND DISABLING

Certain interruption classes can be masked by setting mask bits in the PSW and control registers. When a mask bit is one, the CPU is enabled for a class of interruption; i.e., the interruption is accepted by the CPU and the hardware performs all functions associated with the handling of the interruption. When the mask bit is zero, the hardware handling of the interruption is kept pending until the mask bit is set to one except in the case of certain machine check interruptions which are either ignored or cause the CPU to enter the check-stop state. The CPU is said to be in a disabled state when the mask bit is zero, and the interruption is said to be pending if it is handled after enablement.

The CPU can be disabled for the following type of interruptions:

o   External

o   I/O

o   Machine check

The CPU cannot be disabled for SVC and restart interruptions; in regard to program interruptions, certain subclasses can be disabled by setting mask bits (e.g., overflows in fixed point and decimal arithmetic operations).

4.10 PRIORITY OF INTERRUPTIONS

During the execution of a unit of operation (an instruction or a part of an interruptible instruction) several interruption conditions can take place. For example, an instruction may cause SVC and machine check interruptions and also an I/O or external interruption may be waiting to be serviced after the execution of the instruction. The architecture specifies a priority in which multiple interruptions are presented to the processor.

An exigent machine check interruption is assigned the highest priority, and owing to the nature of this interruption, the acceptance of subsequent interruptions depends on the severity of the hardware error. Assuming there are no exigent machine check interruptions, the priority of presentation of interruptions is in the following order:

o   SVC

o   Program

o   Repressible machine check

o   External

o   I/O

o   Restart

The hardware handles the SVC interruption first, program interruption next and so forth. The operating system's interruption handler can change, by means of disabling, the actual order of presentation of concurrent interruption requests in certain cases.

5. Channel Architecture

5.1 PRINCIPLES OF I/O OPERATIONS

The 370 architecture provides a common framework for performing I/O operations on a variety of devices. In a large scale system, several hundred devices may be present for performing storage and transfer of data. These devices may include disk units, tape drives, printers, and synchronous and asynchronous communication terminals. Each device has its own control characteristics: a tape has to be rewound, a CRT's cursor has to be positioned, and a disk head has to perform a seek operation.

The 370 architecture provides a uniform methodology for interaction between (1) channel and device (2) channel and CPU and (3) channel and main storage.

Typical (and somewhat simplified) interactions between CPU, main storage, channel, control unit and device are schematically illustrated in Figure 5-1. We shall describe the flow of events shown in the diagram in some detail. The CPU issues a Start I/O instruction for starting an I/O operation. The program that issues the Start I/O instruction is usually the operating system's I/O Supervisor. The CPU must be in the supervisor state before it can execute any I/O instructions. ˉefore issuing the Start I/O instruction, a set of channel command words (the set is also called a channel program) has to be created and placed in main storage. A channel command word (CCW) is an instruction to the channel for performing a specific operation and is discussed in detail later on. A Channel Address Word (CAW), which is in a fixed location in real storage, contains the address of the first CCW. The channel fetches the first channel command word (CCW) from the main storage, decodes it, selects the control unit and device (whose addresses are specified as operands in the Start I/O instruction), and sends the control unit the command code contained in the CCW. The control unit

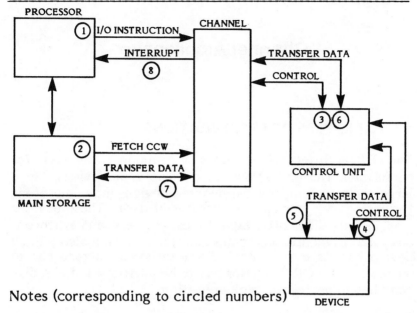

Notes (corresponding to circled numbers)

1. CPU initiates channel operation by issuing an I/O instruction.
2. Channel fetches channel command words (CCWs) from main storage.
3. The channel decodes each CCW and sends the command in the CCW to the control unit.
4. Control unit asks the device to perform the desired command.
5. Data is transferred one bit at a time between device and control unit.
6. Data is normally transferred one byte at a time between control unit and channel.
7. Channel transfers data directly to main storage, without CPU intervention.
8. Channel interrupts CPU at the end of data transfer.

Figure 5-1/Channel Operation

responds with an initial status byte to the channel which the channel, in turn, presents to the CPU. The Start I/O operation ends after presentation of the initial status and the CPU is free to execute other instructions. The I/O operation, however, is not yet complete and the channel fetches the remaining CCWs from main storage, one at a time. It decodes each CCW and issues commands to the control unit. The commands can be for controlling a device (e.g., positioning the read/write head of a disk) or for data transfer (e.g., reading or writing a record from a disk). Depending on the implementations of the channel, device, and control unit, the device may disconnect from the channel while the device performs control functions prior to data transfer. Data transfer takes place between device and main storage, with the channel and control unit providing a path for the data transfer. The channel does not use virtual storage addressing and dynamic address translation in performing storage operations; instead, it uses a technique called channel indirect data addressing (CIDA), which is described later on, in conjunction with virtual storage operations. When the last CCW in the channel program has been executed, the channel presents the CPU with an I/O interruption to indicate completion of the I/O operation. The interruption handler passes control to the I/O Supervisor module of the operating system, which, in turn, passes control to the program that requested I/O operation.

The rest of this section shall deal with specific details of channel types, instructions, commands, and interrupts. The execution of an I/O operation will be spelled out in detail later on; several examples of I/O operations are also given in the chapters dealing with device and control unit implementation.

5.2 CHANNEL TYPES AND THEIR ATTRIBUTES

The architecture specifies three types of channels:

o   Selector

o   Byte Multiplexer

o Block Multiplexer

The byte multiplexer channel is generally used for connecting low speed devices (printer, card reader, card-
punch) while the block multiplexer and selector channels
are used for connecting high-speed devices (disks and high
speed tapes) as shown in Figure 5-2. The word "multiplexer" denotes an important characteristic of block
multiplexer and byte multiplexer channels, namely the
concurrent execution of I/O operations pertaining to
multiple devices. The selector channel, in contrast, performs only one I/O operation at a time and is dedicated to
the device for the duration of the operation. Figure 5-3
shows the recommended channel types for various devices. (Note: UCWs mentioned in Figure 5-3 are explained
in the section on subchannels.)

Selector Channels. These channels are used for high speed
data transfer from devices. Several devices can be connected to a channel, but the channel is dedicated to a
device from start to end of the channel program, even
during the execution of channel commands which cause no
data transfer to take place. (Note that this is not the case
with block multiplexer channels where the device disconnects from the channel when the device is performing
control functions such as positioning a read/write head.)

The characteristics of selector channels are summarized
below:

1. The channel performs only one I/O operation at a time.

2. The channel is attached to a device for the entire
    duration of I/O operation (i.e., the selector channel has
    only one subchannel).

3. The channel is used in connection with high-speed tape
    drives and direct access storage devices (DASD).

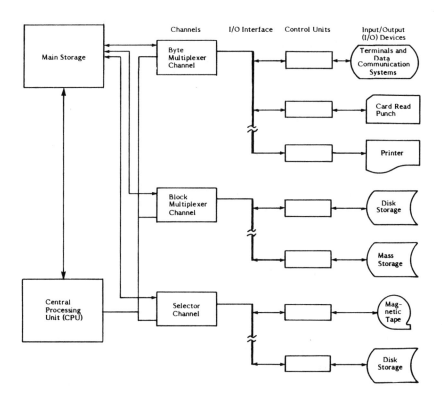

Figure 5-2/System 370 Channel Configurations

I/O DEVICE OR CONTROL UNIT	CHANNEL ATTACHMENT CAPABILITY	RECOMMENDED CHANNEL TYPE	RECOMMENDED UCW MODE WHEN BLCOK MULTIPLEXER MODE IS USED
CARD READERS, CARD PUNCHES, AND PRINTERS			
1442/1443	BYTE, SELECTOR, BLOCK	BYTE	NONSHARED
2501/2520	BYTE, SELECTOR, BLOCK	BYTE	NONSHARED
2821/3811	BYTE, SELECTOR, BLOCK	BLOCK	NONSHARED
3505/3525	BYTE, SELECTOR, BLOCK	BLOCK	NONSHARED
MAGNETIC CHARACTER READERS			
1419	BYTE	BYTE	-
3890	BYTE, BLOCK	BLOCK	NONSHARED
OPTICAL CHARACTER READERS			
1287/1288	BYTE, BLOCK	BYTE	NONSHARED
3886	BYTE, SELECTOR, BLOCK	BYTE	NONSHARED
DISPLAYS			
2250/2840	BYTE, SELECTOR, BLOCK	BYTE	SHARED (SELECTOR MODE)
3272	BYTE, SELECTOR, BLOCK	BLOCK	SHARED (BLOCK MULTIPLEXER MODE)
3036	BYTE, SELECTOR, BLOCK	BYTE	SHARED (BLOCK MULTIPLEXER MODE)
MAGNETIC TAPE			
2803	SELECTOR, BLOCK	BLOCK	SHARED (SELECTOR MODE)
3803	SELECTOR, BLOCK	BLOCK	SHARED (SELECTOR MODE)
DIRECT ACCESS STORAGE			
2314/2319	SELECTOR, BLOCK	BLOCK	SHARED (SELECTOR MODE)
2835 MODEL 1	BLOCK	BLOCK	NONSHARED
2835 MODEL 2	BLOCK	BLOCK	NONSHARED
2841	SELECTOR, BLOCK	BLOCK	SHARED (SELECTOR MODE)
3830	BLOCK	BLOCK	NONSHARED
3851	BYTE, BLOCK	BYTE	NONSHARED
COMMUNICATIONS			
2701	BYTE, SELECTOR, BLOCK	BYTE	NONSHARED
3704	BYTE	BYTE	-
3705 - CHANNEL ADAPTER TYPE 1	BYTE	BYTE	-
3705 - CHANNEL ADAPTER TYPE 2, 3, OR 4	BYTE, SELECTOR, BLOCK		NONSHARED

Figure 5-3/Channel/Device Compatibility

4.   The channel is part of the 360 design, is support-
        ed by 370, but not by the 3033 or 3081.

Byte Multiplexer Channels. As mentioned previously,
a byte multiplexer channel is generally used for connecting low-speed devices like card readers, card
punches and printers. The channel is not dedicated to
any single device while performing an I/O operation,
unlike the selector channel. I/O operations pertaining
to several devices are overlapped.

The characteristics of byte multiplexer channels are
summarized below:

1.   The channel multiplexes I/O operations (i.e., it
        performs overlapping I/O operations).

2.   The channel is used to attach card reader, print-
        er, card punch, 3270 units, 3705 (emulation
        mode), and other low speed devices.

3.   The channel interleaves bytes from several
        devices during the course of data transfer.

4.   The channel is part of the 360 architecture, but
        is supported by the 370, 3033, and 3081.

Block Multiplexer Channels. The block multiplexer
channel is used for connecting high-speed devices.
Like the selector channel, it has a high data transfer
rate but, unlike the selector channel, it performs
multiple I/O operations concurrently. The device
disconnects from the channel while the device is
performing a control operation (e.g., positioning the
read/write head) and is free to execute another channel program pertaining to a different device. During
data transfer, the channel stays connected to the
device until data transfer is complete; in other words,
the channel is dedicated to the device for the duration
of data transfer and does not interleave bytes from
several devices like a byte multiplexer channel.

The block multiplexer channel is ideally suited for use
with direct access storage devices (DASD) that have
rotational position sensing (see the chapter on control
unit and device implementation for a definition of
rotational position sensing). The channel is disconnected from the device during the period of rotational
delay and can service another device. When the addressed sector on the first device is approaching, it
reconnects with the channel and a data transfer takes
place; if the channel is busy with the second device,
the first device tries to reconnect after another rotation.

The characteristics of the block multiplexer channel
are summarized below:

1.   The channel can "multiplex" I/O operations (i.e.,
       perform overlapping I/O operations).

2.   The channel is not attached to a device for the
       entire duration of an I/O operation (i.e., it is dis-
       connected from the device at certain stages of
       the I/O operation).

3.   The channel is used to attach DASD, high speed
       tapes, and sometimes a 3705 communications
       controller.

4.   The channel cannot perform data transfer opera-
       tion to more than one device at the same time
       (i.e., data transfer is not multiplexed); however,
       control operations (e.g., performing a seek) to
       other devices can be overlapped with data trans-
       fer to one device.

5.   The channel is part of the 370 architecture and is
       supported by the 370, 3033 and 3081.

Subchannels. Associated with a channel, there is the
notion of a subchannel; for example, a byte multiplexer connected to several I/O devices may be performing
data transfer from several devices in a byte-inter-

leaved manner and, in such a case, a subchannel is associated with each device. A subchannel is a set of registers within the channel for recording addresses, byte count, and status and control information associated with each I/O operation that the channel is in the process of executing. Thus, a selector channel has only one subchannel because it executes only one I/O operation at any given time. Both byte multiplexers and block multiplexers can have several subchannels.

A subchannel may be shared by several devices or used exclusively by a single device. When the subchannel is shared by several devices, only one device is logically connected to the subchannel for the duration of an I/O operation. A subchannel may thus be viewed as a logical entity for controlling an I/O operation. The physical entity in the channel that corresponds to a subchannel is the Unit Control Word (UCW). For instance, in the case of a byte multiplexer channel, a table of 256 UCWs is stored within the channel. The UCW contains the address, count, and status and control information pertaining to an I/O operation. A shared UCW in a block multiplexer channel can also be assigned one of two modes, either selector or block multiplexer. Figure 5-4 shows the relationship between subchannels, UCWs and devices.

The sharing of a subchannel by various devices is accomplished by assigning UCWs to devices during system installation. A UCW is designated as shared or non-shared, and in the case of a shared UCW, a set of contiguous addresses is assigned to the devices that are shared by the UCW; if the UCW is not shared, only one device is assigned to it, and this device has a unique UCW. If there are no shared UCWs, every device attached to the channel has a unique UCW associated with it.

5.3 I/O INSTRUCTIONS

An input/output operation is initiated by an I/O instruction executed by the CPU.

o   Subchannel -- the channel resources used in performing
     a single I/O operation. Many channels perform several
     concurrent I/O operations and a subchannel is
     associated with each operation. Multiplexing is
     possible only when a channel has several subchannels.
     Channels have internal registers for storing address,
     count, status, and control information pertaining to an
     I/O operation. These registers are called unit control
     words (UCWs). A subchannel is associated with a
     UCW.

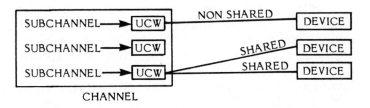

1.   Unit Control Words (UCWs) are registers that are
     stored in a channel (or in a director) and a UCW
     contains address, count, status, and control
     information pertaining to an I/O operation in progress.

2.   A UCW is assigned to a device by the channel on an as-
     needed basis.

3.   Multiple devices can be assigned to a UCW by explicit
     assignment during initialization of the channel.

Figure 5-4/Subchannels within a Channel

There are nine instructions under this category: Start I/O, Start I/O Fast Release, Test Channel, Test I/O, Halt I/O, Clear I/O, Clear Channel, Halt Device, and Store Channel ID. Each instruction format contains the operation code, the channel address, and the device address (which includes the control unit address also) as shown in Figure 5-5. All channels, control units and devices have addresses which are specified at system generation (see Appendix 1) and which do not change during program execution.

Start I/O (SIO). This instruction is used for initiating an input/output operation that involves sensing the status of a device, controlling the device and data transfer between device and main storage.

On execution of this instruction, the channel reads the contents of the Channel Access Word (CAW) at location 72 of main storage. It is the responsibility of the program that issues the SIO instruction, normally the I/O Supervisor of the operating system, to load location 72 with the correct CAW.

The format of the CAW is shown in Figure 5-5. The CAW contains two fields used by the channel, namely a storage protection key and the address of the first Channel Command Word (CCW). The storage protection key is matched with a key for a 2K-storage block whenever reference is made to a main storage location during the I/O operation. The address of the CCW is used by the channel to read the first CCW.

The format of the CCW is shown in Figure 5-5. The CCW contains a command code, the address of the first byte of data that is to be transferred, six flags, and the number of bytes to be transferred (byte count).

The flags in the CCW indicate whether any one of the following features are present: data chaining (DC), command chaining (CC), suppress length indication (SLI), skip (SKIP), program controlled interruption (PCI), and indirect data addressing. We shall discuss

OPERATION CODE	CHANNEL ADDRESS	DEVICE ADDRESS

0   16   24   31

(a) I/O INSTRUCTION FORMAT

STORAGE PROTECTION KEY	0 0 0 0	CCW ADDRESS

0   4   8   31

(b) FORMAT OF THE CHANNEL ACCESS WORD (CAW)

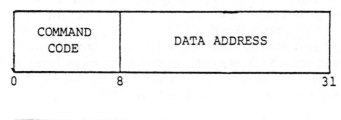

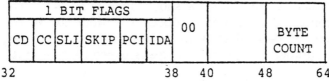

(c) FORMAT OF THE CHANNEL COMMAND WORD (CCW)

Figure 5-5

these features later on in this section.

The Start I/O instruction is initiated if (a) subchannel and device are available and (b) the channel is either available or in the interruption-pending state and errors have not been detected. Assuming that channel, subchannel and device are available, the CPU is not released for performing its next instruction until the device is selected.

The condition code in the PSW indicates whether or not the I/O operation has been initiated. An I/O operation is not initiated if the channel or subchannel is busy or if there is an error associated with the device. In the case of error, status bits are stored in the Channel Status Word (CSW).

Start I/O Fast Release (SIOF). This instruction is similar to the Start I/O instruction. It initiates an input/output operation, but it differs from the SIO instruction in the following respects:

1.   It is meant to be used with block multiplexer channels.

2.   It initiates an I/O operation regardless of whether the device is available or not, providing that (a) the subchannel is available and (b) the channel is either available or in the interruption-pending state and errors have not been detected.

The advantage that the SIOF has over SIO lies in the fact that SIOF initiates the I/O operation before device selection and it frees the CPU earlier than the SIO instruction; if the device or control unit is busy, an I/O interruption is subsequently generated by the channel.

Test Channel (TCH). This instruction tests (1) whether the channel is operational or not, (2) whether it is operating in the burst mode, and (3) whether it has pending interrupt condition if it is operating in the burst mode. An explanation of the term burst mode is given in Chapter 10. A condition code is set in the PSW on completion of this instruction. (This instruction is used by performance monitoring routines in MVS to accumulate statistics about how busy a channel is during the course of a specified interval.)

Test I/O (TIO). This instruction is used to check on the status of a channel, subchannel and device. The status is indicated by the condition code in the PSW.

Store Channel ID (STID). This instruction is executed when the following information pertinent to the addressed channel is required: channel type (selector, byte multiplexer, block multiplexer), channel model number, and the maximum I/O extended logout length that can be stored by the channel during an I/O interruption.

Halt I/O (HIO). This instruction terminates the current I/O operation at the device level, subchannel level, or channel level, depending on the address.

Halt Device (HDV). This instruction terminates the current I/O operation of the addressed I/O device; this instruction is used in conjunction with block multiplexer channels, to halt the I/O operation pertaining to a specific device, without interfering with other channel operations in progress.

Clear I/O (CLRIO). This instruction serves the same purpose as Test I/O instruction, and is used instead of the Test I/O in the case of block multiplexer channels.

Clear Channel. This instruction resets the I/O interface connected to the channel, if the channel is not busy doing some I/O operation. A condition code is set to indicate whether the reset was performed or not, and if not, whether the channel was busy or not operational.

5.4 CHANNEL COMMAND WORD

The channel command word (CCW) has the format shown in Figure 5-5. It has four fields: command code, data address, flags, and byte count.

Command Code. There are six channel commands: write, read, read backward, control, sense, and transfer in channel. The command code field is 8 bits in length and the left most bits are called modifier bits. For example, the command code for write is MMMMMM01 where the first 6 bits are modifier bits. The modifier bits are used to issue orders to the device; functions that are unique to a device (e.g., writing home address or writing record zero (R0) in the case of a disk drive as explained in the chapter on disk control unit and drive implementation) are controlled by means of modifier bits.

Data Address. The data address specifies the main storage address of the first byte of data that is to be transferred, except when channel indirect data addressing is specified (in the context of virtual storage operations).

Flag Fields. There are six flags that are pertinent to the execution of channel programs. Figure 5-5 shows the codes used in the flag fields. An explanation of the codes is given below.

Command Chaining (CC). This is a technique used to execute several CCWs using a single SIO or SIOF instruction (see Figure 5-6). If command chaining is indicated in a CCW, the next CCW is fetched by the channel from the double word location that follows the address of the current CCW, after execution of the current CCW. Command chaining is used in setting up channel programs as described in a later section.

Data Chaining (DC). Data chaining is used to transfer data to or from noncontiguous locations (see Figure 5-7) in real storage. When the data chaining flag is on, a

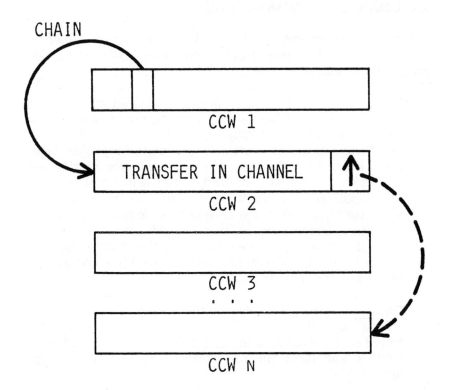

CHAIN

CCW 1

TRANSFER IN CHANNEL

CCW 2

CCW 3

. . .

CCW N

NOTES:

o   If command chaining is indicated, next CCW is as-
     sumed to be at the next doubleword location; an SIO
     operation uses a channel program comprising several
     CCWs, some of which are chained.

o   If a CCW in a non-contiguous location is to be execut-
     ed as part of a channel program, a CCW using a Trans-
     fer in Channel command is used.

Figure 5-6/ Command Chaining

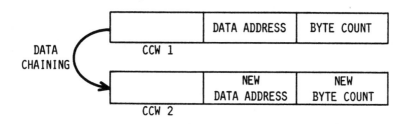

NOTES:

o   Data is normally transferred according to specifica-
    tions in a CCW, namely:

    -    Data Address

    -    Byte Count

o   if it is necessary to transfer data to or from two
    separate real storage locations during a read or write
    command, a data chaining flag is indicated in the
    CCW. After transferring data according to specifica-
    tions in the CCW, a new CCW is fetched from the next
    contiguous location and this CCW contains a new data
    address and a new byte count.

Figure 5-7/Data Chaining

new CCW is fetched from the next successive location when all the data specified by the byte count field of the current CCW has been trasferred. The command field of the new CCW is ignored (unless it is a transfer in channel command) and data transfer takes place using the address specified by the CCW.

Program Controlled Interruption (PCI). In the course of execution of an I/O operation using several CCWs it may be desirable to have an interruption at some intermediate point, and the PCI flag in the CCW causes a CPU interruption. This intermediate interruption does not in any way affect the execution of the current I/O operation, but is a means of notifying the CPU of the progress of the current I/O operation.

The following comments are in order:

1. Normally a channel interrupts the CPU after completion of an I/O operation.

2. The PCI flag in a CCW causes an interruption during or after execution of that CCW.

3. PCI can be used to periodically check the progress of an I/O operation.

Channel Indirect Data Addressing (CIDA). This facility is used in conjunction with dynamic address translation, to transfer data to and from noncontiguous page frames (see Figure 5-8).

When this facility is used, the data address in the CCW is no longer a main storage location but a pointer to a main storage location. The data address field contains the location of the first indirect address word (IDAW) to be used for data transfer. Additional IDAWs are in successive locations in storage. The first IDAW contains the address of a main storage location and data is transferred to or from that location until a 2K byte integral boundary is reached. Then the next IDAW is used. It contains the starting address of another 2K

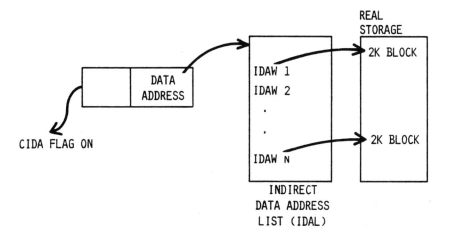

NOTES:

o   A single CCW can be used to control data transfer
    across non-contiguous pages in real storage, by setting
    the channel indirect data addressing flag.

o   If the indirect data addressing flag is on, the data
    address in the CCW is used as a pointer to a list of
    words called indirect data address words (IDAWs) each
    of which contains the absolute address of a 2K byte
    block in storage location.

Figure 5-8/Channel Indirect Data Addressing (CIDA)

block of main storage, and the process is repeated.

The reason for using CIDA is that contiguous page frames in main storage may not be available for data transfer under a virtual storage operating system. For example, assume 8K bytes of data is to be transferred to main storage from a disk. Before issuing the Start I/O instruction, the I/O Supervisor of the operating system page-fixes the buffer for the data transfer (i.e., two not necessarily contiguous 4K pages are allocated in main storage for this operation). CIDA is a convenient technique for indicating that non-contiguous page frames are used in data transfer. The same result can be achieved using data chaining but the difference is that only one CCW is used in CIDA whereas multiple CCWs are used in the case of data chaining.

Skip (SKIP). This flag suppresses data transfer to main storage during the execution of a read, read backward, or sense operation.

Suppress Length Indication (SLI). This flag indicates whether an incorrect length condition is to be indicated at the end of an operation.

Byte Count Field. This field designates the number of bytes of data involved in a data transfer.

5.5 CHANNEL COMMANDS

There are six channel commands, and their codes are given below:

o   Write (MMMMMM01)

o   Read (MMMMMM10)

o   Read Backward (MMMM1100)

o   Control (MMMMMM11)

o   Sense (MMMM0100)

o   Transfer in Channel (MMMM1000)

The M bits serve as modifier bits, and their function is to provide commands that are unique to a device. A list of commands pertaining to operation on a disk drive is given in the chapter on disk control unit and drive implementation (see Figure 12-12).

> Write Commands. Any command byte ending with a 01 sequence is a write command. A device may have several write commands associated with it. In the case of a disk drive, the write commands include search commands and formatting commands as discussed in the chapter on disk storage control unit and drive implementation.

> Read Commands. Any command byte that ends with a 10 sequence is a read command. See Figure 12-12 for an example of read commands pertaining to a disk drive.

> Read Backward Command. This command is initiated by the device and data is transferred from device to main storage. An example of the execution of this command is the backward reading of a magnetic tape unit.

> Control Commands. The command code for control is MMMMMM11 and for many control functions the modifier bits (designated by M) are intended to convey orders to the device.

> In the case of a disk drive, control commands are used for seeking a cylinder or track, for recalibrating the drive, and other such functions described in Figure 12-12.

> Sense Command. This command is used to detect the status of the device and also the conditions detected during the last operation.

Transfer in Channel Command. This command is used
to provide chaining between CCWs that are not located in contiguous double words. The data address field
of this command contains the next CCW address. This
command does not perform any I/O function like the
other commands.

5.6 CHANNEL PROGRAMS

A channel can be regarded as a specialized computer
capable of performing only one function, namely I/O
operation. The channel needs a program to perform this
function, and it is the responsibility of the operating
system to create a channel program before initiating an
I/O operation. The following are the main characteristics
of channel programs:

o   A channel program consists of a collection of chained
    channel command words (CCWs); the address of the
    first CCW is placed in the channel address word (CAW)
    before issuing the Start I/O instruction (see Figure 5-
    9).

o   The channel fetches the first CCW, decodes it and
    executes it; if command chaining is indicated, the next
    CCW is fetched, decoded and executed and the process
    is continued until the last CCW (i.e., a CCW that does
    not contain a transfer-in-channel command and does
    not have a chaining indicator) is processed.

Branching and Looping. A channel program requires
branching and looping capabilities to perform certain
I/O operations. For example, suppose it is desired to
read a record with a specific ID from an IBM 3350 disk
drive. The following steps are involved in such an
operation:

1)   Place the read/write head above the track which
     contains the record to be read (known as a SEEK
     operation).

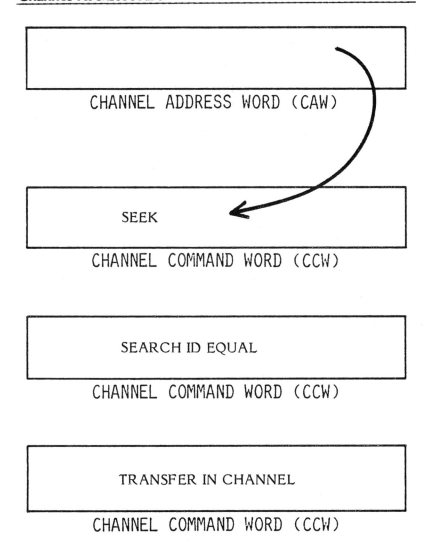

Figure 5-9/Schematic for a Channel Program

2) Read the ID of a record in the track and compare it with the specified ID (known as SEARCH ID operation).

3) If the comparison is unequal, then go to step (2); if the comparison is equal, then go to step (4).

4) Read the contents of the record.

The actual channel program consists of the following commands:

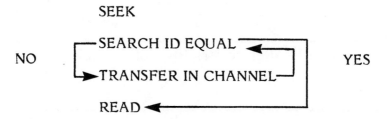

These commands are explained in detail in the Chapter 12. For the time being, we shall concern ourselves with the branching and looping aspects of the channel program. After a SEARCH ID operation, the device notifies the channel whether the comparison was equal or unequal. In the case of an equal comparison, the channel fetches the CCW containing the READ command (i.e., it skips the CCW immediately following the one containing the SEARCH ID EQUAL). In the case of an unequal comparison, the channel executes the next CCW which contains the transfer-in-channel command that loops back to the CCW containing the SEARCH ID EQUAL command.

Notice that the architecture does not explicitly specify the skipping of the next CCW and branching to its successor as a means of exiting from a loop while performing iterative searches. This procedure is used in interaction with disk drives and the reader is referred to Chapter 12.

The important characteristics of channel programs are

described in Figure 5-10.

5.7 I/O INTERRUPTION

The action taken on I/O interruption is illustrated schematically in Figures 5-11 and 5-12. The hardware stores the old PSW in real storage locations 56 through 63, loads the new PSW from locations 120 through 127, and stores the following additional information:

o   Channel Status Word in locations 64 through 71

o   Channel and Device Address in locations 186 through 187

o   Limited channel logout information (in case of error) in locations 176 through 175 and extended logout information in locations whose starting address is given in locations 172 through 175.

The new PSW contains the address of the I/O interruption handler routine which is an operating system module. The details of handling of the interruption depends on the operating system but, in general, the following actions take place:

o   Error-handling operations are performed if an error in the I/O operation is indicated.

o   If there are no errors, the program that initiated the I/O operation is notified of the completion of the I/O operation.

Channel Status Word (CSW). The format of the CSW is shown in Figure 5-13. The CSW is a double word and is always stored at real address location 64. It is available for use until the next I/O interruption occurs or the next I/O instruction causes a change in its contents.

The key field contains a 4-bit storage protection key.

FUNCTION	– To give a channel a list of commands, so that it can perform an I/O operation; each command is contained in a channel command word (CCW) and the channel address word (CAW) points to the first CCW (channel programs are used only in conjunction with start I/O instruction).
CREATION	– Channel programs are created by access methods and by certain operating system routines.
VIRTUAL STORAGE OPERATION	– In general, channel programs use virtual address for data transfer and reside in virtual storage. The I/O supervisor module of the operating system performs the following functions:

    o   Page-fixes data areas (buffers)

    o   If a buffer crosses a page boundary, adds an IDAW to the IDAL.

    o   Translates virtual data addresses to real addresses.

    o   Copies the CCW into fixed real storage and puts real data address into the CCW.

    o   Loads the channel address word (CAW) with the real address of the CCW and issues a start I/O instruction.

Figure 5-10/Channel Programs

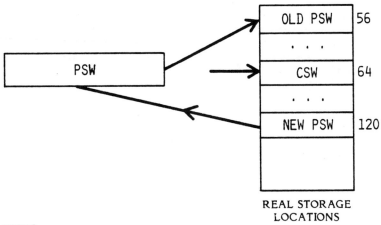

REAL STORAGE
LOCATIONS

NOTES:

o   An interruption by the channel is called an I/O inter-
    ruption.

o   An I/O interruption causes the following hardware
    events:

    -   Contents of PSW are placed in "old PSW location"
        and PSW is loaded with contents of "new PSW
        location."

    -   A channel status word (CSW) is stored into a
        fixed real storage location.

Figure 5-11/I/O Interruptions

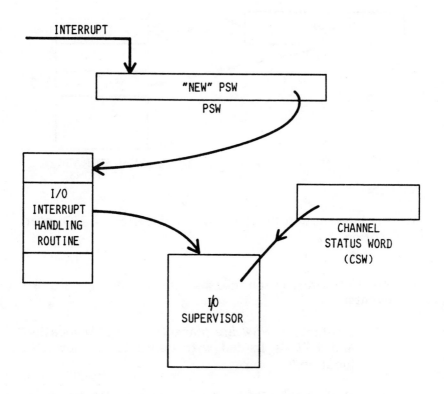

Figure 5-12/Interruption Handling by Software

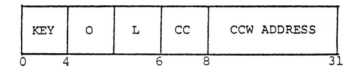

Figure 5-13/Format of the Channel Status Word (CSW)

The L flag (bit 5) indicates that a pending logout condition exists. The cc code (bits 6 and 7) indicate whether or not a deferred condition code for start I/O Fast Release is present. The CCW address field gives an address that is equal to the address of the last CCW used plus eight bytes. Bits 32 through 47 identify the status, and each one of the sixteen bits is used to flag conditions, some of which are listed below.

1)   Channel End.   This condition indicates that the channel has successfully performed its function and that the device does not need the channel any more.   The channel end condition is not generated when errors of malfunctions are detected during the I/O operation.

2)   Device End.   This condition indicates that the device has successfully completed the I/O operation assigned to it by the channel.

3)   Control Unit End.   This condition indicates that the control unit has successfully completed its role in the I/O operation.

4)   Unit Check.   This condition arises from the fact that the I/O device or control unit has noticed an unusual condition which is given in detail as the data given to the sense command.   It can be caused by a malfunction of a device or a program error during the activity associated with an I/O operation.   Command retry procedures are activated using unit check, channel end, and status modifier.

5)   Unit Exception.:   Unit exception does not necessarily mean an error and is to be interpreted in the context of the command and the device.   For instance, recognition of a tape mark can cause a unit exception.

6)   Status Modifier.   This bit is flagged by the device

when it cannot provide its current status while responding to a TEST I/O instruction, if the control unit is busy, or when command retry is to be initiated.

Channel Logout. The channel logout facility is an aid for diagnostic or error recovery purposes in case of noncompletion of an I/O operation caused by channel malfunctioning. There are two sections to the logout, namely a limited channel logout and an extended channel logout. The limited channel logout provides information that is independent of the actual channel model in use. The extended channel logout contains information that is dependent on the actual channel model that is in use. The I/O Communications Area (IOCA) is a 32-byte table contained in real address locations 160 to 191. This table contains limited channel logout information (4 bytes) and, if applicable, a pointer to the extended logout information area. The information contained in the channel logout identifies the storage control unit, the most likely source of error (e.g., CPU, channel, control unit, storage), the type of termination and so forth.

Classification of I/O Interruptions. I/O interruptions can be initiated by a device or channel in a variety of situations, and the Channel Status Word (CSW) contains flag bits indicating the type of interruption. We shall list next the circumstances that cause I/O interruption and describe the actions taken by the channel and device:

1) End of Data Transfer: The control unit and device present the channel with an indication that it has successfully or unsuccessfully executed a CCW in a channel program by means of channel end, device end, unit check, etc. which were discussed earlier. At the end of execution of the CCW that contains a read or write command, the control unit and device present the following indicators on successful completion:

o   channel end

o   device end

The channel checks to see if the channel program has been completely executed (i.e., the last CCW has been processed) and if it has, the channel requests an interruption; if there are remaining CCWs to be executed, the channel does not request an interruption. See Chapter 12, Section 3 for a detailed analysis of channel, control unit and device interaction.

In the case of error in an I/O operation, the device may present a unit check indicator or a unit exception indicator in addition to channel end and device end.

2)   Attention Interruption: This interruption is initiated by a device (or control unit) to indicate that it has unsolicited data to send to a program. The program is notified by the I/O Supervisor that it should start an I/O operation for reading from the device. An example of a device that uses the attention interruption is the locally attached IBM 3270 Display Station which requests this interruption when the attention key is depressed.   Another example is the I⌐M 3705 Communications Controller (under the "native" mode) which uses this interruption when it is ready to transfer data to main storage.

3)   Miscellaneous Channel-Initiated Interruptions: The channel can initiate an interruption in several situations, some of which are listed below:

o   When a CCW contains a program controlled interruption (PCI) flag, the channel presents an interruption request. (PCI is used to periodically check the progress of complex I/O operations such as loading a program from disk storage to main storage.)

o   When the channel encounters program
checks or protection checks or when the
device presents the channel with a unit
check. (A unit check indicates that there is
something wrong with the device and it
cannot proceed with the I/O operation.)

o   In the case of a block multiplexer channel,
if the channel has indicated that it was busy
in response to an I/O instruction, it can
present a Channel Available Interruption
(CAI) when it is free.

The indicators presented by the channel for
various interruption types are summarized in
Figure 5-14.

5.8 PHASES IN THE EXECUTION OF AN I/O OPERATION

We shall now summarize the events that take place during
the execution of a complete I/O operation. There are two
instruction components in the execution of an I/O operation: an I/O instruction and channel commands. The I/O
instruction is executed by the CPU, the channel command
is decoded by the channel, and subsequently passed on to
control unit and device for execution.

In what follows we shall consider the execution of a Start
I/O instruction using a byte multiplexer channel and the
follow-through of the instruction to the point of the I/O
interruption.

Initial Selection Phase. The CPU initiates this phase
with the Start I/O operation which contains channel
and device addresses. The channel fetches the CAW
from a fixed location in main storage. The channel
sends the address of the device to all control units
attached to the channel. A control unit that recognizes the address responds by sending the address in
return. The channel now sends a command (obtained

o   Interruption on I/O completion without errors

-    Channel End (CE) -- Channel has completed an operation and is free for use.

-    Device End (DE) -- Device has completed an operation and is available for use.

-    Control Unit End -- Control Unit has completed an operation and is available for use. Control Unit End is used in conjunction with shared channels and devices.

o   Interruption on I/O related errors

-    Checks -- A check is usually by a malfunction and can apply to a channel, device, or control unit; a check detection normally causes discontinuation of the I/O operation.

-    Exceptions -- An exception denotes an unexpected event (e.g., recognition of a tape mark) and does not necessarily denote an error.

Figure 5-14/Flags Presented on Interruption

from the CCW which in turn is pointed to by the CAW) to the device, and the device returns a status byte to indicate whether or not it can execute the command.

The Start I/O operation is complete at this stage and the PSW and CSW contain condition codes.

Data Transfer Phase. The channel transfers data between device and main storage under read or write commands. An I/O operation may involve transfer to several noncontiguous storage areas. In this case multiple CCWs coupled by data chaining are used to effect the data transfer. When multiple commands are necessary to effect an I/O operation, command chaining is used. Channel indirect addressing is used to support virtual storage architecture.

Data transfer takes place one byte at a time, and the CPU may perform other functions while transfer is in progress.

Conclusion Phase. The normal conclusion of an I/O operation is indicated by the channel end and device end conditions. These conditions are indicated by the Channel Status Word (CSW) which is stored at a fixed location in main storage.

Interruption Phase. Unless the CPU is disabled, the termination of an I/O operation causes an interrupt action to take place which causes the old PSW to be saved and a new PSW to be loaded.

6. Multiprocessing

The 370 architecture provides the capacity for multiple CPUs to share main storage and communicate with each other using instructions for signalling and response. In actual implementation of multiprocessing (e.g., 370/158, 370/168, 3033, 3081) two CPUs are coupled together and we shall assume in our discussion that the number of CPUs is limited to two.

The characteristics of multiprocessing are given below:

o   Two CPUs share main storage, each CPU having its own real storage which is mapped into main storage by a mechanism known as prefixing.

o   The CPUs do not share channels; each CPU can have its own set of channels (called the CPU's channel set) in which case the computer system is called a tightly coupled multiprocessing system.

o   One CPU can have a channel set and the other CPU no channel set (i.e., it does not perform I/O operations) in which case the computer system is called an attached processing system.

o   In a tightly coupled multiprocessing system, channel sets can be switched and the functions of a failing CPU can be taken over by the remaining CPU, thus providing increased system reliability and availability.

o   The CPUs communicate with each other using an instruction called SIGNAL PROCESSOR, which is described later on; when a CPU fails it can send an emergency signal by executing the SIGNAL PROCES-SOR instruction (with a pre-specified operand), and this causes an external interruption on the other CPU.

It should be noted that there is another form of multipro-

cessing known as loosely coupled multiprocessing, which
has different characteristics:

o   One processor is the master (called global processor)
     and controls the activities of all the other processors
     (called local processors) in the system;

o   The processors are connected to each other by means
     of channel-to-channel adapters which provide data
     transfer paths between channels.

o   The processors share a direct access storage device
     (DASD);

o   The global processor controls job scheduling and device
     allocation for all processors.

The architecture does not deal with loosely coupled multiprocessing since its functions do not require any additions
to the conventional single CPU architecture.

We shall next discuss three topics relating to multiprocessing architecture; namely, prefixing, signalling between
CPUs, and serialization among CPUs.

6.1 PREFIXING

We have seen before that, in the case of a single CPU,
data pertaining to the operation of the CPU are stored in
locations of main storage. This data includes the following:

o   Interruption codes

o   CAW

o   CSW

o   "old" PSWs

o   "new" PSWs

The architecture allocates, in the case of a single CPU, the first 4K byte locations in main storage known as Prefixed Storage Area (PSA) for storing data that is used by CPU for control and operational purposes.

In the case of multiprocessing, it is obvious that both CPUs cannot use the first 4K byte locations in main storage for this purpose because one CPU may destroy the data necessary for operation of the other CPU. A different 4K location is therefore assigned to each CPU and a distinction is made between the addresses used by CPU and absolute main storage address, as explained below.

The 24-bit address used by the CPU is called the real address. Each CPU assumes that the first 4K byte locations of main storage are available to it as PSA and behaves as though it were a single CPU in making storage references. The real addresses are translated by hardware into different absolute storage addresses, as explained next.

Each CPU is given a new register called the Prefix Value Register (PVR). The PVR contains a 12-bit address portion (corresponding to the locations 0 through 4095) which is matched against bits 8 through 19 of the 24 bit address generated by the CPU. The translation of real address to absolute address proceeds as follows:

1) If bits 8 through 19 of the address generated by the CPU are all zero, (i.e., the address is within the range 0 through 4095), they are replaced with the PVR contents; this is known as forward prefixing.

2) If bits 8 through 19 of the address generated by the CPU are not all zeros, (i.e., the address is greater than 4095) and do not match the address portion in the PVR, no change is made to the address.

3) If bits 8 through 19 of the address generated by the CPU are equal to the contents of the PVR, they are set to zeros; this is known as reverse prefixing.

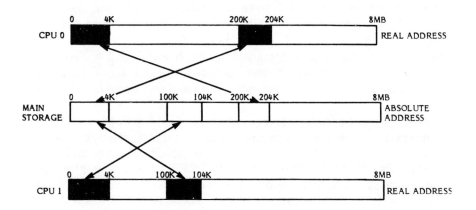

NOTES:

1. Shaded areas in the real address range shows that the real address is different from the absolute address and the mapping between the two is indicated by arrows.

2. The diagram is not drawn to scale, as regards the range of addresses.

Figure 6-1/Real to Absolute Address Mapping
Using Prefixing

In other words, if (1) R is the real address used by the CPU and (2) P is the binary number obtained by appending 12 zeros to the 12-bit address portion contained in the PVR, then R is converted to an absolute address A using the following algorithm:

1) If R is less than 4K, A = P + R

2) If R is greater than or equal to 4K but less than P, A = R.

3) If R is greater than or equal to P but less than P + 4K, A = R - P.

4) If R is greater than or equal to P + 4K, A = R.

Note that the setting of actual values in the PVR for each CPU is a function of the operating system. The architecture provides instructions for loading and storing the contents of the PVR.

An example of prefixing is illustrated schematically in Figure 6-1. There are two CPUs which we shall denote by 0 and 1. Each CPU has a real address range of 0 to 8 MB.

The prefix values for CPU 0 and CPU 1 are 200K and 100K, respectively. Figure 6-1 shows the actual mapping of real storage for each CPU into absolute storage. For CPU 0, a real address in the 0 to 4K range is mapped into absolute locations 200 to 204K; likewise, a real address in the range 200 to 204K is mapped into an absolute address range of 0 to 4K. The real address and absolute address are the same in the ranges between 4K and 200K and between 204K and 8 MB.

Prefixing, as described above, is performed after dynamic address translation. In other words, the sequence of conversions from virtual to absolute addresses takes place as follows:

1) The virtual address is converted to a real address by means of dynamic address translation.

2) The real address is converted to an absolute address by means of prefixing.

6.2 SIGNALLING BETWEEN CPUS

A new instruction called Signal Processor instruction (SIGP) is used for inter-CPU communication. The CPU that generates a SIGP is called the sender, and the CPU that receives the SIGP is called the receiver. The following list shows some of the orders that are issued by the sender via the SIGP instruction:

1. SENSE -- The receiver sends its status to the sender.

2. START -- The receiver enters the operating state if it is in the stop state.

3. STOP -- The receiver enters the stop state if it is in the operating state.

4. STOP and STORE STATUS -- The receiver enters the stop state and the status is saved in absolute storage locations 216 through 512.

5. Initial Microprogram Load (IML) -- The receiver does an initial program reset and performs IML.

6. RESET -- The receiver performs a reset.

7. RESTART -- The receiver begins program execution by fetching a new PSW and storing the old PSW.

8. EXTERNAL CALL -- An external interruption is sent by one CPU to another as a request to provide services (known as "shoulder tapping").

9. EMERGENCY SIGNAL -- An external interruption is presented to the receiver.

The section on 3033 implementation describes hardware aspects of signalling implementation and the reader is referred to it for details.

6.3 SERIALIZATION AND SYNCHRONIZATION

The architecture presents an elaborate set of protocols dealing with serialization among CPUs. In a multiprocessing environment where both CPUs access the same main storage, it is necessary to have conventions regarding the usage of common areas of storage. The MVS operating system has a software mechanism known as a "lock" which allows only one CPU to access common data areas. Each CPU checks a lockword contained in main storage before accessing the common data areas. If the lockword is zero, the CPU stores a CPU identifier into the lockword and the other CPU has to wait until the first CPU is done and stores a zero back into the double word.

A compare and swap (CS) instruction is used in conjunction with operation of locks. The CS instruction has three operands -- a register R_1 , a storage location S_2 , and a register R_3 . The contents of R_1 is compared against the contents of storage location S_2 and (1) on equal comparison, the contents of R_3 are stored in location S_2 and (2) on unequal comparison, the contents of S_2 are loaded into R_1. The results of the CS instruction is given by settings of the condition code.

The CS instruction is an example of an instruction which causes serialization among CPUs. When one CPU is using the CS instruction, the other CPU cannot access the main storage location specified by S_2 . The architecture specifies several other instructions which cause serialization among CPUs; we shall not discuss them here, and the interested reader can consult reference (1.1).

The architecture also specifies instructions for synchronizing time of day (TOD) clocks in the two CPUs. Such synchronization is necessary since difficulties arise if the two clocks show different times. A SET CLOCK instruction is provided to ensure clock synchronization, and an external interruption occurs when the clocks are no longer in synchronization.

6.4 CONCLUDING REMARKS

It is not our intention to provide a very detailed account of the 370 architecture since the definitive work on the subject is IBM's "System/370 Principles of Operation." The treatment of certain topics has been skimpy because they are primarily of interest to implementors of the architecture; on the other hand, certain topics have been explained in greater detail than in the "System/370 Principles of Operation," especially in the area of functions provided by the operating system.

REFERENCE MATERIAL AND FURTHER READING

1.1   IBM System/370 Principles of Operation
      (GA22-7000-6)

      This is the IBM reference manual for the 370 archi-
      tecture, providing a complete definition of 370
      machine instructions.

1.2   "Architecture of the IBM System/370," Case, Richard
      P. and Andris Padegs, Communications of the ACM,
      January 1978, Volume 21, Number 1, pages 73-96.

      This article discusses the 370 architecture using the
      360 architecture as a background frame of reference.

1.3   IBM System/370 System Summary: Processors
      (GA22-7001-10)

      A concise reference source listing the hardware and
      software features of IBM Processors.

PART II
IMPLEMENTATION OF LARGE SCALE
IBM PROCESSORS

7. Concepts Used in Implementation

IBM System 370 processors constitute a family of medium to large scale computers. The smallest of the 370 processors is the 115 which supports up to 384 KB of main storage and has a processor cycle time (which is defined later) of 480 nanoseconds. A large scale processor, like the 3033, on the other hand, supports up to 32 MB of main storage, has a processor cycle time of 57 nanoseconds and can execute 5 million instructions per second (MIPS). The large scale processors in the 370 family include the 370/158, 370/168, 3031, 3032, 3033 and 3081. The implementation of these processors vary in several respects. We shall discuss the implementation of the 3033 and 3081 in the next two chapters and compare it with the 370/168 Model 3 implementation. The reason for doing this is that the 370/168 design is similar to the 3033 design, which in turn has points of similarity with the 3081 design. The salient features of large scale processors of the 370 family are the following:

o   Low cost Metallic Oxide Semiconductor (MOS) memories

o   Storage interleaving

o   Dynamic address translation (DAT) hardware

o   High-speed cache memory

o   Multiprocessing capability

o   Attached processing capability

These features were made available by IBM over a period spanning a number of years. In 1970, the 370 models 155 and 165 were introduced and they used the System/360 design. They had none of the features listed above with the exception of cache memories that were already in use in the 360/195. In 1972, IBM introduced models 158 and 168, having MOS memories, virtual storage and dynamic address translation hardware and in 1973 IBM announced tightly-coupled and loosely coupled multiprocessing systems for the 158 and 168 models.

The IBM 303X (X = 1,2,3) series made their appearance in 1977. The design of the 3033 is similar to that of the IBM 370/168. In fact, as we shall see in a later section, the IBM 3033 can be regarded as a "tuned" version of the IBM 370/168 model 3.

The IBM 3081 was introduced in 1980, and it has two tightly coupled multiprocessors called a dyadic processor. It uses the architectural extensions used in the IBM 3033 and its operational characteristics are somewhat similar to a tightly-coupled multiprocessing IBM 3033 system.

There are several concepts used in the implementation of large scale processors that are not described in the 370 architecture. According to the architecture the logical components of a computer are the following:

o   Central Processing Unit (CPU)

o   Main Storage

o   Channels

o   Control Units

o   Devices

The implementation of the smaller processors (e.g., the 370/138) does conform to a large extent to the architectural model. For instance, the major physical components of the 370/138 are a CPU, main storage and channels. The CPU fetches instructions from main storage one instruction at a time (there is no prefetching) and executes the instruction using microcode resident in reloadable control storage (RCS) which is part of the CPU. The channels function according to architectural specifications even though the 370/138 implementation calls for the sharing of control storage, arithmetic and logical unit between CPU and channels. (This means that when the channel is transferring data the CPU has to wait, thus resulting in a significant loss of computing power when a large number of I/O operations are required.)

The large scale computers (e.g., the 370/168, 3031, 3032, 3033, 3081) while conforming to the overall concepts laid down in the 370 architecture, introduce several functional components that are not mentioned in the architecture. These computers use implementation concepts that are listed below:

o   Cache (High Speed Buffer)

o   Interleaved Storage

o   Instruction Fetching Unit

o   Execution Unit

o   Dynamic Address Translation Unit (mentioned in the architecture)

o   Overlapped Operations

The functions of the CPU are carried out by the Instruction Fetching Unit, Execution Unit, Dynamic Address Translation Unit and High Speed Buffer (cache). The term CPU is sometimes used in describing collectively the above hardware elements (e.g., in the case of the 370/168); but the term processor is also used in describing the above hardware elements plus main storage and sometimes even channels (e.g., in the case of the 3033). In the following paragraphs we shall explain the function of the various elements listed above, and we shall use the words "CPU" and "processor" interchangeably except when a precise distinction is required. (In such a case we shall specify the components that are collectively described by the term "processor.")

7.1 CACHE MEMORIES (HIGH SPEED BUFFERS)

A cache memory (also called a high speed buffer) is a small high speed memory used in storing prefetched instructions and operands. The cache memory is not addressable by programs and is physically distinct from main storage. The access to cache memory is made via hardware, and a cache search is done by hardware before accessing main storage.

The rationale for having a cache memory can be understood by a comparison between CPU and main storage speeds. The time required for execution of an instruction by the CPU is usually a fraction of the time required for bringing the instructions from main storage. For instance, the 3033 executes several instructions in two processor cycles, each processor cycle having a duration of 57 nanoseconds (see the section on processor and memory cycles for a definition of these terms); on the other hand, the read/write cycle time for memory operations is 285 nanoseconds. Hence, a 64K cache memory that can be accessed in one processor cycle is used to avoid waits by the CPU on main storage operations; instructions and data pertaining to program execution are fetched in advance from main storage (anticipating the needs of the executing program) and stored in the cache.

A detailed account of the operation of the cache memory is given later, in the section on IBM 3033 implementation. The functional aspects of cache memory are described in Figures 8-7 and 8-8.

7.2 INTERLEAVED MAIN STORAGE

The architecture views main storage as a collection of bytes that have sequential address starting from zero. Nothing is mentioned regarding the interaction between main storage and its two users, namely the CPU and channels. For instance, assume that a channel is transferring data to main storage. Can the CPU or another channel access main storage at the same time? The architecture leaves these decisions to implementation; the interaction between processor, channel, and main storage depends on the implementation.

Storage interleaving is a design concept used in the implementation of the large scale computers in the 370 family (e.g., the 168, 3033, 3081). When interleaving is not used, main storage can satisfy only one read/write request at a time; in other words, if a channel is transferring a byte of data to main storage, the CPU has to wait before accessing main storage. This is the case with smaller processors in the 370 family (e.g., the 138 or 158). When interleaving is used, multiple concurrent requests to main storage is possible. This is because main storage is organized into several independently accessible units called logical storage elements (LSEs). If there are n such LSEs, main storage is said to be n-way interleaved. The 370/168 model 3 uses 4-way interleaving, and the 3033 uses 8-way interleaving. The CPU and channels can make concurrent requests to main storage, provided the byte addresses are in different LSEs. For example, assume that the LSEs are numbered from 0 to 3 (in the case of the 370/168 model 3); then a CPU can access a byte in LSE 0 while the channel is concurrently transferring data to a byte in LSE 1. Note that contention occurs if both CPU and channel address the same LSE. Usually the channel has precedence over the CPU in such a situation.

For an example of interleaved storage operation, the reader is referred to the section on processor storage under IBM 3033 implementation; functional descriptions of interleaved storage operations are given in Figures 8-3 to 8-5.

7.3 INSTRUCTION FETCHING UNIT AND EXECUTION UNIT

We shall first take a look at the typical operations performed by a CPU in the course of instruction execution. A list of such operations is given below:

o   Instruction fetching

o   Instruction decoding

o   Operand fetching

o   Dynamic address translation

o   Instruction execution

In the case of large scale processors, the above operations are not necessarily performed in the sequence listed above.   Instructions are prefetched and decoded by an Instruction Processing Unit (I-Unit) in the case of the 370/168, 3033, and 3081. A detailed description of the I-Unit is given in the section on 3033 implementation. The I-Unit has its own buffers which are filled from the cache memory on a look-ahead basis; access to main storage is made only if there is a cache miss (i.e., the cache does not contain the required data).

The I-Unit passes decoded instructions to an Execution Unit (E-Unit) in the case of the 370/168 and 3033. The E-Unit contains registers, PSW and microcode used in instruction execution.   A detailed description of the E-Unit is given under the section on implementation of the IBM 3033.

7.4 PROCESSOR CYCLES AND MEMORY CYCLES

The notion of a processor cycle is of utmost importance in understanding the internal behavior of processors.   A processor initiates operations relating to instruction fetching or execution at the start of a cycle.   In other words, the processor uses discrete time intervals for initiating and performing its work.   These time intervals are called processor cycles.

The processor can begin one or several operations at the start of a cycle, depending on the extent of instruction overlap incorporated in the design; also, an instruction can be executed in one or several cycles, depending on the design of the processor.

Memory operations (read and write) are initiated at the

start of a processor cycle. The time interval required to complete a memory operation is known as the memory cycle. Processor cycles are of smaller duration than memory cycles. For instance, in the case of the 3033 the processor cycle is 57 nanoseconds while memory cycle is 285 nanoseconds.

7.5 OVERLAPPED OPERATIONS (PIPE-LINING)

The processor does not remain idle while memory operations are in progress; instead, it performs various other operations pertaining to fetching, decoding and translation of instructions. As a matter of fact, the processor initiates several operations at the start of a processor cycle. For example, it can initiate the fetching of instructions from the cache, issue a read or write instruction to main storage, and start executing an instruction which is present in the Execution Unit's waiting queue. Thus, the processor performs many overlapped operations during a processor cycle. Specific examples of such overlapped operations are given in the section on the IBM 3033 implementation (see Figure 8-11).

8. IBM 3033 Processor Implementation

In this chapter we shall describe the details of the implementation of the IBM 3033 Processor. First we shall list the significant features of the 3033 and explain key concepts used in the implementation.

The IBM 3033 processor has the following characteristics:

o It has a processor cycle time of 57 nanoseconds; during a cycle, instruction fetching and execution operations are overlapped.

o The processor has an 8-way interleaved main storage that can vary in size from 4 MB to 32 MB.

o The processor has 64 KB high speed buffer (cache memory) that has an access time equal to the processor cycle time.

o The processor can have a maximum of 16 channels (12 standard, 4 optional).

o Channels are organized into groups; each group has a director that has its own microcode and arithmetic logic circuitry for performing channel oeprations.

o Two processors can function in a tightly coupled multiprocessing mode (MP) or attached processing (AP) mode.

o The processor supports the 370 Extended Facility (microcode to support MVS) and has several optional features, discussed later.

There are three models of the 3033, indicated by suffixes U, N and S. What we shall discuss in this section is the implementation of model U. Models N and S have the same structural organization as model U, but they do not have the performance capability of the model U. For instance, model N has only four-way storage interleaving and 16 KB cache memory; model S also has four-way interleaving and only 1/2 KB of cache memory. Both models N and S can be field-upgraded to model U.

8.1 OVERVIEW OF THE PROCESSOR

The word "processor" is used to collectively describe the following items:

o Instruction Unit   called Instruction Preprocessing Function (IPPF)

o Execution Unit

o Main Storage (called Processor Storage)

o Processor Storage Control Function (PSCF)

o Channels

o Channel Directors

o Maintenance Retry Function

A stand-alone 3033 processor is called a uniprocessor. Two 3033 processors can be configured to form a tightly coupled multiprocessing configuration. Also, a processor without channels can be attached to a uniprocessor to form an attached processing configuration.

Figure 8-1 illustrates the major components of the processor; note that the PSCF contains the following sub-components:

o High Speed Buffer (cache)

o Translation Lookaside Buffer (TLB)

o Dynamic Address Translation (DAT)

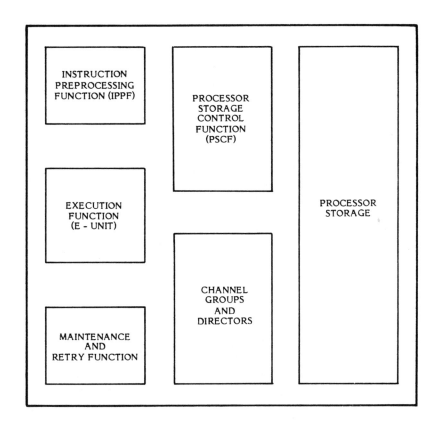

Figure 8-1/Components of the 3033 Processor

o   Segment Table Origin (STO) Stack

We shall discuss the functions of each of these elements in later paragraphs.

A simplified flow diagram (Figure 8-2) shows the main sequence of events (numbered circles) in the processor. The IPPF prefetches instructions from the cache memory in the PSCF, and stores them in its buffers (Event 1). IPPF decodes the instructions one at a time and prefetches operands (Event 2) using the Translation Lookaside Buffer (TLB), the Dynamic Address Translation (DAT) feature, cache, and main storage. Main storage is divided into 8 logical storage elements (for 8-way interleaving). The instructions are placed in a queue for execution (Event 3) and are executed in sequence by the Execution Unit. In the case of I/O operations, the Execution Unit gives I/O instructions to channels and data transfer is done between channel and main storage (Events 4 and 5).

8.2 PROCESSOR STORAGE

The size of processor storage varies from 4 MB to 32 MB in increments of 4 MB. Storage is divided into 8 logical storage elements (LSEs). Each LSE can be accessed independently of other LSEs to achieve 8-way storage interleaving. Contention for an LSE occurs when two components of the processor attempt to access the same LSE and is resolved in favor of the component with the higher priority; for instance, a request from a channel is given preference to a fetch request from the IPPF.

A double word (eight bytes) is the basic unit of storage access from each logical storage element (i.e., the data path to and from processor storage is 8 bytes wide) and 8 double words can be requested from 8 LSEs concurrently, each request separated by one processor cycle (57 nanoseconds) from its predecessor. The bytes are numbered according to the following convention: bytes 0 to 7 are in LSE 0, bytes 8 to 15 are in LSE 1, bytes 16 to 23 are in LSE 2 and so forth, as shown in Figure 8-3. Figures 8-4 and 8-5 describe processor storage features and memory opera-

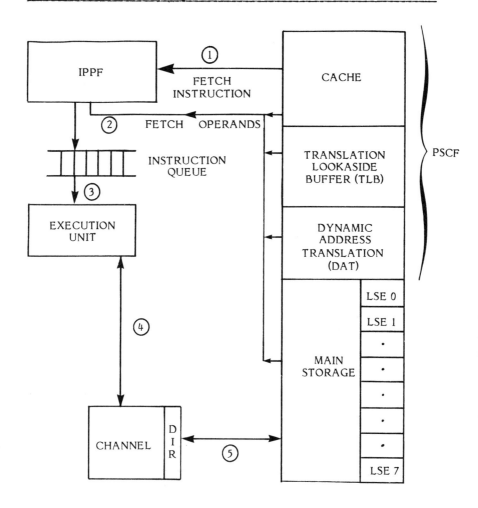

NOTE: Numbered circles are events which are described in the text.

Figure 8-2/Simplified Flow Diagram Showing 3033 Processor Operation

INTERLEAVED PROCESSOR STORAGE

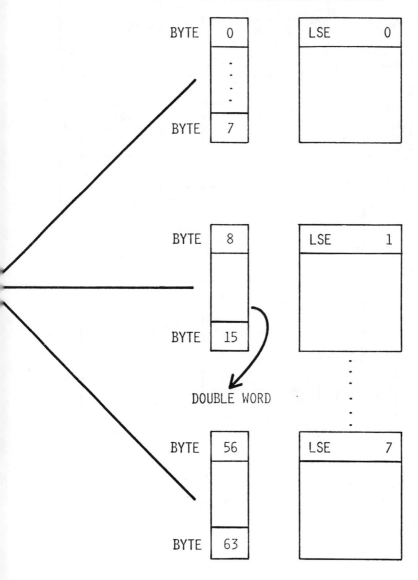

Figure 8-3/Interleaved Processor Storage

tions.

Storage Protection. A 7 bit key for each 2K byte of storage is used for storage protection, as specified in the architecture. Before an LSE is accessed, a storage protection check is made via special hardware called a storage protect array.

Error Checking and Correction (ECC). Special hardware provides for the detection and correction of one-bit errors and for the detection of all two-bit and several multi-bit errors.

8.3 PROCESSOR STORAGE CONTROL FUNCTION (PSCF)

The Processor Storage Control Function consists of the cache, the dynamic address translator, the translation look-aside buffer, the channel bus controller, and the segment table origin address stack. In general, PSCF controls all access to processor storage, as shown in Figure 8-6.

8.3.1 High Speed Buffer (Cache)

The 3033 uses a 64 KB high speed buffer (cache) for storing instructions and data during program execution. A simplified description of the cache is given in Figure 8-7.

The use of a 64 KB cache is one of the reasons for the high performance of the 3033 processor. The cache has the same cycle time as the processor (57 nanoseconds): a double word can be obtained from the cache in 2 processor cycles, and a request for a double word can be initiated during every processor cycle. The Instruction Preprocessing Function Unit (IPPF) can thus obtain a double word from the cache in 114 nanoseconds as compared to 285 nanoseconds if no cache were used.

Organization. The cache is organized as a matrix having 64 columns and 16 rows. Each of the 64 x 16

o   Size: 4 MB to 32 MB.

o   READ/WRITE Cycle Time: 285 nanoseconds.

o   Data Path Width: 8 Bytes

This means that 8 Bytes (i.e., a double word) are brought in during one READ Cycle and also are written out to Main Storage during a WRITE Cycle.

o   Storage Interleaving -- 8 Way

This means that there are 8 banks of memory which can be independently accessed by the Processor; each memory bank is called a logical storage element (LSE) and is numbered from 0 to 7.

Figure 8-4/3033 Processor Storage Features

o   Main storage is divided into 8 independently accessible LSEs.

o   Only one LSE can be accessed during a Processor Cycle.

o   An LSE can be accessed only if it is not busy; "busy" means it is working with another request.

o   An LSE can be accessed by:

Channel

Processor

o   Channel has priority over the Processor, if both request the same LSE.

o   The Unit of Transfer between LSE and Processor is a double word (i.e., path width between Processor and Storage is 8 bytes).

o   A double word from each LSE can be accessed in 8 consecutive Processor Cycles.

o   When less than a double word is to be stored, a double word is read from storage, merged, and rewritten to storage.

Figure 8-5/3033 Main Storage Operations

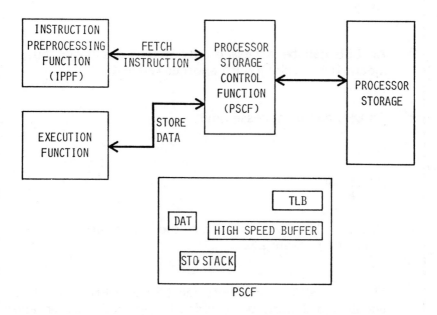

Figure 8-6/Processor Storage Control Function

o   What it is -

   -   A high speed temporary storage area having a size of 64K bytes used for anticipatory storage of instructions and data during program execution.

o   What it is not -

   -   It is not part of processor storage.
   -   It is not addressable by operating system programs or application programs.

o   Cache "hit" and cache "miss" -

   -   A cache "hit" takes place when data needed by the IPPF or Execution unit is found in the cache; a cache "miss" takes place when data is not found in the cache.
   -   In the case of a cache miss, 8 double words are obtained from processor storage; these 8 double words are placed in the cache, replacing 8 existing double words in the cache (a "Least Recently Used" algorithm is employed for this purpose).

o   Its impact on performance -

   -   A double word required from main storage is found 92% of the time in the cache.
   -   A double word can be fetched from the cache in 2 processor cycles (114 nanoseconds); a double word can be fetched from processor storage in 285 nanoseconds (without cache search) and 456 nanoseconds (with cache search).

Figure 8-7/Functional Description of High Speed Buffer (Cache) Used by the 3033 Processor

(≈1024) elements of the matrix is called a block and consists of 8 double words or 64 bytes.

A block is the basic unit of data in cache operation. The cache search scheme (described in the next paragraph) initially looks for a block and then for the double word within the block. The transfer of data between cache and main storage is eight double words at a time; i.e., main storage is also viewed in terms of 64 byte blocks for data transfer purposes.

Interrogation. When the IPPF or E-unit wants a double word from main storage, the cache is interrogated to find out if it contains the double word. The real address of the double word is used for interrogation and an address array is used for searching the cache, as schematically illustrated in Figure 8-8. The address array has 64 columns and 16 rows. Each element contains a 13-bit address, a block valid bit, and a block delete bit. The procedure for checking to see if a double word is in the cache or not is given below (the numbers in the procedure correspond to circled numbers in Figure 8-8):

1. Obtain column address from bits 20 through 25 of the real address (6 bits correspond to 64 columns).

2. Compare each of the sixteen elements in the column of the address array to see if there is a match for bits 8 through 20 of the real address against the 13 bit address field.

3. If a match exists and if the valid bit is one, go to the corresponding block in the cache and obtain the appropriate double word specified by bits 26 through 28 of the real address; otherwise, load a block from main storage.

Transfer of data from main storage. A replacement array having 64 elements is associated with the cache to maintain a record of the least recently used blocks. The cache tries to keep active data in storage

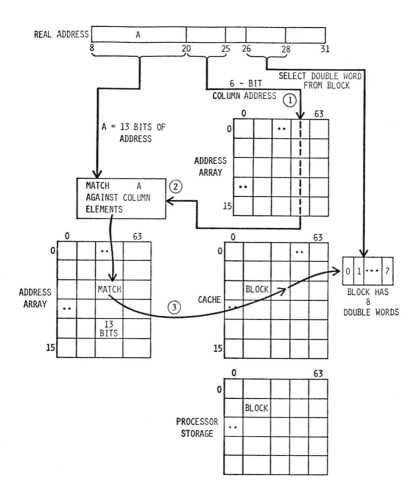

Note: Circled numbers are events described in the text.

Figure 8-8/Operation of the Cache

and the replacement array contains, for each column of the cache, indicators of block usage.

When the requested double word is not in the cache, a block is read from main storage by transferring 8 double words using 8 storage references, one cycle apart. Processor storage is viewed logically as consisting of blocks for the purpose of data transfer to the cache; in other words, processor storage is regarded as having 64 columns and n rows, where n is dependent on the available processor storage (n = 1000 if processor storage is 4 MB). Each block has 8 double words, as in the case of the cache, and a cache miss results in the transfer of a block.

Store-Through Operation. When processor storage is to be updated by means of a store operation by the processor, the cache is interrogated to see if it contains the double word in question and, if it does, both cache and processor storage are updated (otherwise only processor storage is updated).

Interaction with Channels. Channels do not read from cache but directly from processor storage. In the case of an update to processor storage, the cache is also interrogated; if it contains the double word to be updated, the whole block is invalidated by setting the invalid bit in the corresponding element in the address array.

8.3.2 Dynamic Address Translation (DAT)

The dynamic translation facility used in the 3033 conforms to the specifications laid down in the 370 architecture.

Virtual storage is organized hierarchically into address space, segment, page and byte. An address space can have a maximum size of 16 MB, a segment can be 64 KB or 1 MB and a page can be either 2 KB or 4 KB.

The translation process is similar to the one described in the chapter on architecture. Figure 8-9 shows schematic-

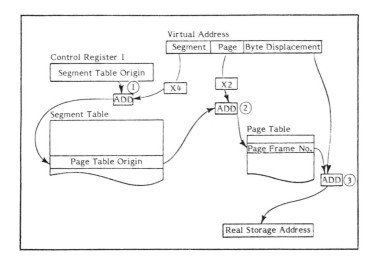

NOTES CORRESPONDING TO CIRCLED NUMBERS:

1. Add (segment index times 4) to the segment table
    origin to get the page table origin: an entry in the
    segment table is 4 bytes long.

2. Add (page index times 2) to the page table origin to
    get the page frame address; each entry in the page
    table is 2 bytes long.   (NOTE: The page table entry
    may not contain the address and the invalid bit may be
    one, in which case a page fault results).

3. Add byte displacement to the page frame address to
    get the real storage address.

Figure 8-9/Dynamic Address Translation

ally the dynamic address translation process, with 4K page and 64K segment conventions.

8.3.3 Translation Lookaside Buffer (TLB)

Dynamic address translation takes 10 to 40 processor cycles, depending on whether segment and page tables are in the high speed buffer or in processor storage. TLB makes it possible to cut down requests for dynamic address translation.

The TLB is used to hold up to 128 previously translated page addresses. Every time DAT translates a virtual address to a real address, the following information is kept as one of the 128 TLB entries:

o   real address (bits 8 through 20) of the page frame

o   virtual address (bits 8 through 14) of the page

o   storage protection key (SP)

o   segment table origin stack ID

In order to understand the significance of the entries kept in the TLB, we shall recapitulate the addressing conventions used in virtual and real storage. A 24-bit virtual address has a segment index, page index and byte index as shown in Figure 3-3. To translate this to a real address, only the segment and page indices need be converted (i.e., bits 8 through 19, assuming a 64 KB segment and 4 KB page) since the byte index does not change under a virtual to real address translation (see Figure 3-7 also). The TLB stores bits 8 through 19 of the real address, which corresponds to the address of a page frame. Only bits 8 through 14 of the virtual address are stored because of the hashing scheme employed in TLB interrogation which is described later.

The segment table origin (STO) stack ID is required when the operating system supports concurrent execution of multiple virtual address spaces. The virtual-page to real-page frame correspondence contained in the TLB is meaningless unless the ID of the address space to which the virtual page belongs is also specified. The STO stack ID performs this identification function, as explained in a later section.

TLB Interrogation. The TLB can be viewed as a table having 64 entries, as shown in Figure 8-10. The A and B sections are identical, and the Least Recently Used (LRU) array indicates whether A or B is in use during a given time interval.

The inputs for the interrogation are the virtual address and the currently active STO Stack ID. The TLB is searched using the following algorithm:

1) Using a hashing technique on bits 9 through 20 of the virtual address, obtain a number k ranging from 0 to 63 corresponding to the 64 TLB entries.

2) Check the LRU array to determine whether section A or B should be used.

3) Obtain the kth entry from the TLB using the appropriate section.

4) Check if the virtual address bits 8 through 14 in the TLB entry match the corresponding bits of the virtual address which is used for searching the TLB.

5) If the two sets of address bits match, and the STO IDs are the same, the real address is formed using bits 8 through 19 in the TLB and concatenating it with the byte index.

6) If the two sets of address bits do not match, or the STO IDs are not the same, the real address is not in the TLB and dynamic address translation has to be performed.

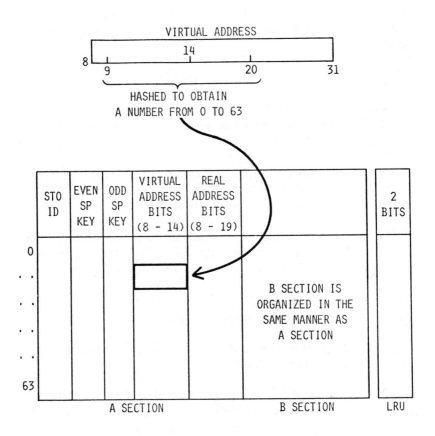

Figure 8-10/Operation of the Translation Lookaside Buffer
(TLB)

The TLB search is done in parallel with cache search. Only two processor cycles are required to fetch a double word, assuming that the double word is cache-resident and its virtual address is in the TLB; Figure 8-11 explains the TLB/cache parallel search operation.

8.3.4 STO Stack

The function of the Segment Table Origin (STO) Stack is to enable TLB searches to be made in a multiple virtual storage environment. Figure 8-12 depicts the information carried by the STO Stack. Every address space that is executing within the system is given a STO Stack ID. Before the execution of an address space, control register 1 is loaded with a segment table address and control register 0 is loaded with segment and page size information by the operating system. Whenever control register 1 is thus loaded with the segment table address, the hardware checks to see if the STO stack has the segment table address; if it has, the corresponding STO Stack ID is designated as being active. If there is no match, new entries for segment size, page size, and table entries are created and the corresponding STO Stack ID is designated as being active.

The interrogation of the TLB includes the matching of the STO Stack ID in the TLB with the currently active ID to ensure that the real address belongs to the current virtual address space that is being executed.

8.4 INSTRUCTION PREPROCESSING FUNCTION (IPPF)

The IPPF prefetches instructions, decodes instructions, makes address calculations, and prefetches operands. The prefetched instructions are stored in 3 instruction buffers, each buffer having a size of 32 bytes (see Figure 8-13). This means that, on an average, 24 instructions can be stored in the buffers. The instructions are found in the cache for about 92 percent of the fetches. A cache miss involves a fetch from main storage.

1. Assume that the Instruction Preprocessing Function Unit (IPPF) wants a double word to be fetched, whose virtual address is specified.

2. Logically, the following steps have to be taken in sequence:

    2.1   Obtain real address of the double word

          -    Search TLB

          -    If not in TLB, use DAT

    2.2   Search cache, using real address

    2.3   If not found in cache, fetch from processor storage

3. The 3033 performs parallel operations processing and only 2 processor cycles (114 nanoseconds) are required to get the required double word under the following conditions:

    o   A TLB Entry exists for the virtual address

    o   An entry exists in the cache for the real address found in the TLB.

Figure 8-11/TLB/Cache Search Parallel Operation

ID #	SEGMENT SIZE	PAGE SIZE	SEGMENT TABLE ADDRESS

VARIES FROM
2 TO 30

Note: One STO ID is denoted as being active at any given time, corresponding to the address space that is being executed.

Figure 8-12/Segment Table Origin (STO) Stack

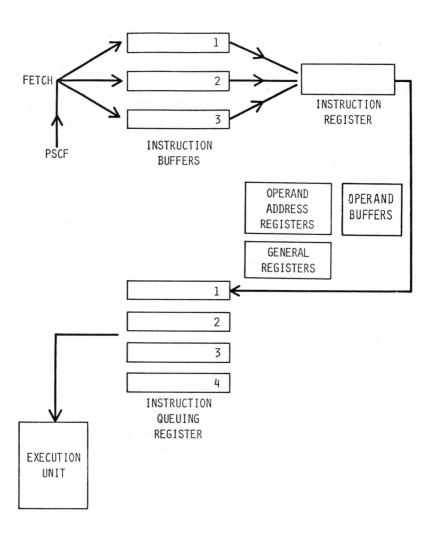

Figure 8-13/Schematic Diagram for the Instruction
Preprocessing Function (IPPF)

The three instruction buffers are used to prefetch instructions along the paths taken by branches in a program. At any one point in time, one of the buffers is designated as active and the other two as idle. Instructions are decoded from the active buffer and, in the case of a branching instruction, an idle buffer is filled with instructions from the branched-to point and becomes the active buffer after the branching instruction is decoded. In case of a conditional branch, a guess is made as to the most likely outcome of the instruction and an idle buffer is filled with instructions starting from the point that the program is likely to branch to. This idle buffer is then activated and the decoding of instructions follows along a path based on the most likely outcome of branches. The third buffer is used for storing instructions in the same manner if a second branch is encountered before a resolution has been made in respect to the first branch.

The instruction register holds an instruction while it is being decoded. A decoded instruction is placed in a queue, using an instruction queuing register. Up to four decoded instructions can be placed in a queue waiting for execution. Instruction decoding and operand address generation are done in the same cycle.

The general registers in the IPPF are similar to those mentioned in the architecture and are used exclusively for making address calculations by the IPPF. The operand address registers and buffers are used for prefetching operands.

8.5 EXECUTION FUNCTION (E-FUNCTION)

The Execution function executes instructions from the System/370 instruction set, one instruction at a time. It is capable of processing a new instruction on every processor cycle, and several instructions (nearly half of the instruction set) can be executed within one such cycle. The E-function initiates I/O operations, loads new PSWs after interruptions, and performs many functions related to program execution. Microprograms control various E-function operations. These microprograms are resident in

a control storage which is not accessible to other programs. The logical components of the E-function are the
following:

o   general registers

o   control registers

o   PSW

o   timer facilities

o   storage control unit

Figure 8-14 illustrates the organization and functions of
the Execution Unit. The general registers, control registers, PSW, and timer facilities are the same entities that
are described in the chapters on architecture.

8.6 CHANNELS AND DIRECTORS

The 3033 channels are physically part of the processor; the
channels are divided into groups of six and four, and each
group is controlled by a director. Each channel group in
the 3033 (there are two such groups) consist of one-byte
multiplexer channel and five-byte multiplexer channels.
An extended channels feature is available for adding
another group of four channels, of which one may be a byte
multiplexer and the other three block multiplexers or, all
four may be block multiplexers (see Figure 8-15).

Each director and channel operates under its own microcode, and a director shares control storage with the channels associated with it. Figure 8-16 shows the organization
of a director schematically. Each director has its own
arithmetic logic unit for channel and data control functions, channel buffers, storage for UCWs associated with
channels, and local storage.

The block multiplexer channels within a director are
controlled by a microprogram that is shared by all channels
as well as by special hardware controls. The following

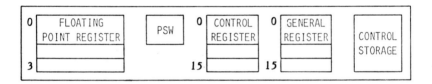

Figure 8-14/Schematic Diagram for the Execution Unit
(E-Unit)

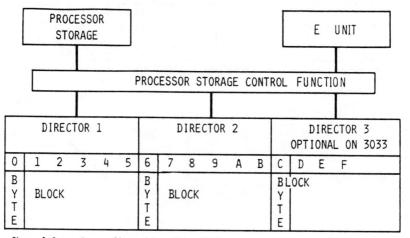

Channel C can be configured as either BYTE or BLOCK.

Figure 8-15/Channel Implementation in the 3033

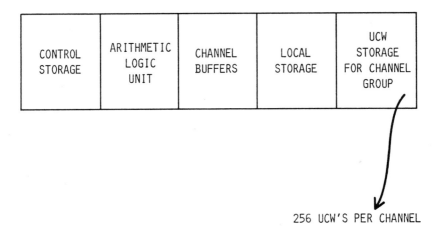

Figure 8-16/Schematic Diagram for Channel Director

channel functions are performed under microprogram control:

o   CCW fetching under command chaining

o   Data transfer to and from processor storage

o   Initial device selection

o   I/O interruption

Specialized hardware is used for certain functions associated with control units, namely reselection and data transfer via the I/O interface. (See the chapters on control unit and device implementation for an explanation of these functions.) Each channel has dedicated hardware buffers and this, coupled with the multiprogrammed director, makes it possible that data transfer by one channel does not significantly interfere with the operations of another channel.

The byte multiplexer is handled by a different microprogram within the director and performs all channel functions other than device selection. Also, this program can be interrupted by a block multiplexer channel when it needs service by the director.

Data Flow. A device transfers data to the channel via the control unit one byte at a time. (A two-byte interface can be installed in the first block multiplexer channel in a group, and in this case two bytes are transferred at a time between channel and control unit.)

The channel transfers four bytes at a time to the registers contained within the director and this data is transferred to processor storage via the PSCF (see Figure 8-17). The transfer from processor storage to registers in the director is done eight bytes at a time and the channel transfers data to the device one byte at a time (or two bytes if the two-byte interface is installed). The maximum aggregate data rate achieved by the five block multiplexer channels within a director is 6.7 MB per second. When all three directors are used, the maximum aggregate data rate for fourteen block multiplexer channels is 18.9 MB per second. These numbers are given with a view to show the maximum overall data transfer rates between the processor and devices and to illustrate the I/O throughput capability of the 3033.

Cache Invalidation. If the contents of processor storage locations are also cache-resident, the contents of the cache block are invalidated in the case of channel operations that involve reading from a device.

Channel Control. As mentioned previously, the directors control all channel activity such as channel-to-storage data transfer and device selection. The starting of an I/O operation follows the rules given in the 370 architecture, namely:

o   The CPU (i.e., the E-Unit) issues an I/O instruction (SIO or SIOF).

o   The channel and device address are specified as operands in the I/O instructions. (The address of the director is not specified in the instruction.)

o   A channel program is executed by the channel.

o   The CPU (i.e., the E-Unit) is interrupted on completion of an I/O operation or whenever such an interruption is necessary (as in the case of Program Controlled Interruption).

8.7 MAINTENANCE AND RETRY FUNCTION UNIT

This unit handles interaction between a console and the processor; it also provides for instruction retry. The 3033 has the ability to retry an instruction in case of an error or failure. Data that is altered by an instruction is saved beforehand, and error-handling microcode restores the E-Unit to a point where the instruction can be re-executed.

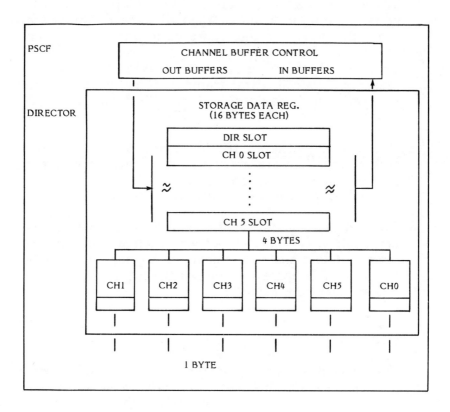

The channels are handled in a multiprogrammed manner by a microprogram within each director, with the block and byte multiplexer channels being handled by different subprograms. The path width from storage to channels is 8 bytes, from channels to storage 4 bytes, from the director's registers to channels 4 bytes, and those to the outside world are 1 byte (although the first block multiplexer of any group may have a 2-byte wide path.)

Figure 8-17/Data Flow in the Director

8.8 MULTIPROCESSING

The following types of multiprocessing are supported by the 3033 processors:

o   Tightly coupled multiprocessing (MP)

o   Attached processing (AP)

o   Loosely coupled multiprocessing

We shall describe the characteristics of each type next.

Tightly coupled multiprocessing. Under tightly coupled multiprocessing (called the MP mode) two processors share main storage and run under a single operating system. Each processor has its own set of channels which can be switched from a failing processor to the functioning processor by means of special instructions (Channel Disconnect, Channel Connect). The two processors do not share channels but can share control units and devices if the control unit has channel-switching capability and if the device has string-switching capability. Channel-switching and string-switching are explained in the chapter on control unit and device implementation. For the time being, we shall only note that channel-switching is the capability of a control unit to switch channels, and string-switching is the capability of a set of disk drives (called a string) to switch control units; the underlying motivation here is to provide multiple I/O paths to a device so that more than one processor can access the device.

The schematic components in a multiprocessing configuration are illustrated in Figure 8-18. The two processors are connected with each other via specialized hardware called a 3038 Multiprocessor Communications Unit (MCU). The MCU performs the following functions for both processors:

o   Prefixing

o   Storage access

o   Broadcast of storage update

o   Interprocessor communication

o   Configuration control

Each of these functions is described below.

Prefixing. We have seen in the chapter on architecture that each processor generates real addresses
which have to be mapped to absolute addresses by
means of prefixing. The first 4K locations used by
each processor (called the Prefix Storage Area) is
assigned to different areas in processor storage by
means of offsets contained in prefix registers. Prefixing has been described in chapter 6 and the reader is
referred to it for details.

Storage Access. Access to shared storage is controlled
by the MCU. Each processor has to go through the
MCU to read or write to main storage, and this results
in a slight increase in storage access time. Eight-way
storage interleaving is still used. Requests to a non-
busy LSE is granted on a first-come, first-served
basis. When both processors make simultaneous requests, a floating priority scheme is used whereby
storage access is granted in bursts. One processor is
allowed to have priority over the other processor if it
can keep up a continuous request (e.g., a 64 byte fetch)
but if it fails to do so, priority passes to the other
processor.

Broadcast of Storage Update. If one processor updates
processor storage, we have seen that its cache is also
updated by means of a store-through technique. In a
multiprocessor environment, when one processor
updates storage, the hardware automatically broad-
casts this to the second processor and, if its cache
contains data that is affected by the update, such data
is automatically invalidated. Note that data transfers

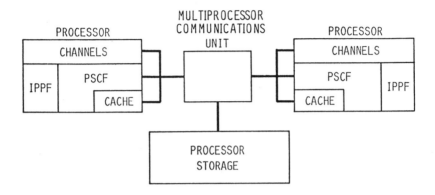

1. Two processors share storage and run under one operating system.

2. Both processors communicate with each other and access storage via the Multiprocessor Communications Unit.

3. Each processor owns its set of channels, but one processor's channel set can be switched to another (e.g., in the case of failure of a processor).

4. Two processors can share (but need not) devices, providing the devices and control units have channel switching and/or string-switching features.

Figure 8-18/Tightly Coupled Multiprocessing

to main storage by channels are also treated in this
manner. Also, when one processor modifies a storage
protect key (by means of the SET STORAGE KEY
instruction) the other processor is also notified of this
modification and makes changes accordingly.

Interprocessor Communication. Interprocessor communication is done by means of the SIGNAL PROCES-
SOR instruction as well as by special hardware. As we
have seen in the chapter on architecture, the SIGNAL
PROCESSOR instruction enables one CPU to send
signals to the other CPU. These signals can be used by
one processor to start, stop, or sense the status of the
other processor and to perform several other functions
which have been described already.

Specialized hardware is used in notification of malfunction alert, whereby an external interruption is
generated in one processor if the other processor
enters into a check stopped state either on account of
loss of power or machine failure. This hardware is also
for synchronization of time-of-day (TOD) clock facilities.

Configuration Control. Processor storage can be
configured in three ways, namely:

-    Each processor has its own storage and the other
     processor cannot have access to it (self-con-
     tained configuration).

-    One processor can have exclusive use of parts of
     the other processor's storage (cross-configura-
     tion).

-    Processor storage is shared by both processors
     (shared configuration).

In general, symmetric as well as asymmetric configurations are supported under multiprocessing. A symmetric configuration is one where there is processor
symmetry, storage symmetry, and I/O symmetry. By

processor symmetry we mean that both processors have the same features and are interchangeable. Storage symmetry means that each processor has been assigned identical amounts of main storage which is shared by both processors. I/O symmetry means that each processor has identical channel sets which share all devices by means of channel switching. A configuration that does not satisfy these criteria is called asymmetric. In practice, most MP configurations are asymmetric because a substantial operating system overhead is required in sharing devices necessitated by I/O symmetry.

Attached Processing. Attached Processing (called AP mode) is similar to tightly coupled multiprocessing, the only difference being that one processor (called the Attached Processor) generally does not have any channels of its own.

The two processors are coupled by means of the Multiprocessing Communication Unit (MCU) which performs the function described previously.

Attached processing can be regarded as an example of asymmetrical multiprocessing since only one processor performs I/O operations. Channel set switching is possible between processors by means of CONNECT CHANNEL SET and DISCONNECT CHANNEL SET instructions.

Attached processing is used instead of multiprocessing when extra CPU power is required to meet the processing demands of a computer system.

8.9 OPTIONAL FEATURES

The 3033 has certain optional features which we shall discuss briefly. The first feature is called "Extended Addressing." What this means is that the CPU can address more than 16 MB of real storage; in fact, a uniprocessor or attached processor can address up to 24 MB of real storage. In a tightly coupled multiprocessing environment up to 32 MB of real storage can be addressed. Note that the virtual address space size is still 16 MB, as specified by the 24-bit architecture. Extended addressing is used by the MVS/System Product operating system for improving paging operations.

Another optional feature is the two-byte interface which enables data transfer of two bytes at a time (instead of the usual one byte at a time) between channel and control unit. This feature can be installed on block multiplexer channels and doubles the transfer rate between channel and device. A third feature, called data streaming, allows block multiplexer channels to be connected to control units using increased cable lengths (of up to 400 feet) while permitting a transfer rate similar to that obtained with a two-byte interface.

8.10 COMPARISON WITH THE IBM 370/168 (MODEL 3)

The IBM 3033 design is similar to the IBM 370/168 (Model 3) in many respects. Figure 2-19 shows the major components of the 370/168 system, namely the Central Processing Unit and channels.

The Central Processing Unit (CPU) includes the following items:

o   Instruction Unit (I-Unit)

o   Execution Unit (E-Unit)

o   Processor Storage

o   Processor Storage Control Function (PSCF)

Note that channels are housed separately from the Central Processing Unit and are connected to the I/O Channel Control in the PSCF by means of a dual bus having a data path width of 8 bytes (Figure 8-19).

The PSCF consists of the following items:

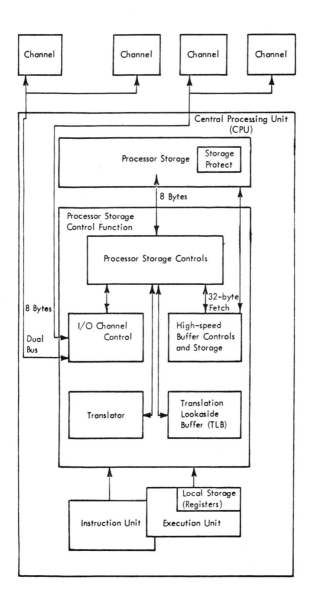

Figure 8-19/Organization of the 370/168

o   Dynamic Address Translation Hardware (DAT)

o   High Speed Buffer (cache)

o   Translation Lookaside Buffer (TLB)

o   I/O Channel Control

o   Processor Storage Controls

The Instruction Unit (I-Unit) fetches and decodes instructions and operands and provides a queue of decoded instructions for the Execution Unit as in the case of the 3033. The I-Unit has two instruction buffers instead of the three used in the 3033 implementation. Instructions are prefetched from the cache and stored in the instruction buffers. Instructions are decoded from one of the buffers called the "active" buffer, operand addresses are generated, and operands are fetched. In the case of a branching instruction, the remaining buffer is filled with instructions along the branch path; if the branch is conditional, one of the buffers is designated as active by means of a guess based on design experience and decoding follows along the most likely branch path. The Execution Unit (E-Unit) executes instructions one at a time from the queue created by the I-Unit and uses microcode for this purpose.

Processor storage is four-way interleaved (as compared to eight-way interleaving in the 3033), and access to storage by CPU or channels is controlled by the PSCF. The PSCF has a 32 KB cache which is used for prefetching instructions and operands.

The channels do not have directors (as in the case of the 3033) and the I/O Channel Controls element in the PSCF controls and processes channel requests. Each channel is allocated two buffers in the I/O Channel Controls element, each buffer holding a double word. One buffer is used for outbound data transmission, and the other buffer is used for inbound data transmission. Each buffer transfers data to and from an interleaved unit in storage.

The 370/168 supports the byte multiplexer, block multi-plexer and selector channels. (Note that the selector channels are not supported by the 3033 or 3081.)

9. IBM 3081 Processor Implementation

The salient features of the IBM 3081 processor are given below:

o It consists of two central processing units (called central processors) in a tightly coupled multiprocessing mode; if one central processor fails, the other processor can take over its functions but the failed processor cannot be repaired immediately and the repair has to be deferred while the system functions in a degraded mode with one central processor. The two processing units cannot be decoupled to function as two uniprocessors, as in the case of the 3033 MP, and the two processing units are collectively referred to as a dyadic processor.

o It uses the 370 architecture, with the following 3033 extensions made to the architecture:

   - extended addressing (see Optional Features of 3033)

   - data streaming (see Optional Features of 3033)

o The central processor cycle is 26 nanoseconds (compared to 57 nanoseconds for the 3033).

o The central storage can be 16 MB, 24 MB or 32 MB and is shared by the two processors.

o Sixteen or twenty-four channels are assigned to two channel sets, one channel set per processor.

The 3081 Processor Unit comprises the following elements, as shown in Figure 2-20:

o Two Central Processors

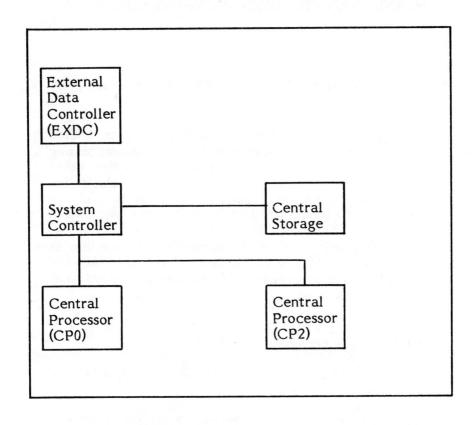

Figure 9-1/Organization of the 3081 Processor

o   Central Storage

o   System Controller

o   External Data Controller

9.1 PROCESSOR OVERVIEW

Each Central Processor consists of the following units:

o   Instruction Element (IE)

o   Variable Field Element (VFE)

o   Execution Element (EE)

o   Control Storage Element (CSE)

o   Buffer Control Element (BCE)

We shall give brief descriptions of the functions of each of these units.

Instruction Element. The instruction element (IE) not only prefetches instructions but also executes the majority of instruction types (e.g., shift, branch and logical instructions). It has its own buffers, registers and instruction execution is under microcode control. The functions of IE are listed below:

-   It prefetches instructions.

-   It controls the sequencing of all instructions.

-   It initiates all storage requests arising in the course of instruction fetching and execution.

-   It executes instructions having RR, RRE, RX, RS, S and SI formats.

-   It handles interruptions.

Variable Field Element (VFE). The VFE executes SS and SSE instructions. It has a decimal adder, two input registers and two output registers. The VFE operates under microcode control.

Execution Element (EE). The EE executes only certain types of instructions, namely fixed point division and multiplication, conversion from binary to decimal and vice versa, and floating point instructions.

Control Storage Element (CSE). This element contains microcode used during program execution and also general and control registers used by each Central Processor.

The microcode is also resident in central storage in an area called the System Area. Frequently used microcode is kept in the CSE, and infrequently used microcode is kept in the System Area. The transfer of microcode from the System Area to the CSE is referred to as "microcode page-in."

Buffer Control Element. The Buffer Control Element (BCE) contains a 32 K byte cache memory, dynamic address translation (DAT) hardware, a translation lookaside buffer which is called Directory Lookaside Table (DLAT), and a directory for the cache that keeps track of modifications of the rows (also called lines or blocks) of the cache and other miscellaneous information. A cache miss results in 16 doublewords being transferred from central storage.

The BCE handles all references to central storage by the central processors. A central processor does not directly read from or write to central storage (as in the case of 3033) but always uses the cache for this purpose.

9.2 CENTRAL STORAGE

Central storage size can be 16, 24 or 32 megabytes. A portion of central storage is reserved for microcode (at least 262 KB) and is not accessible to programs. This reserved area is called the System Area which contains, in addition to microcode, unit control words (UCWs) for I/O devices and various tables and directories. The remainder of central storage is addressable by means of storage reference instructions and is equivalent to main storage as specified in the 370 architecture.

The following list describes the main features of central storage:

o   Storage is organized into independent units called basic storage elements (BSEs).

o   Each BSE is divided into two basic storage modules (BSMs).

o   Storage is two-way interleaved in the sense that contiguous 2K byte blocks can be independently accessed.

o   A double word is the basic data unit for memory operations (i.e., the data width is 8 bytes).

o   Error checking and correction (ECC) code bits are stored as part of data in central storage; single bit errors are corrected but multiple bit errors are only detected.

o   Storage protection is carried out according to architectural specifications, and the system controller contains the storage protection array.

9.3 EXTERNAL DATA CONTROLLER (EXDC)

The EXDC is responsible for all I/O operations as it manages the activity of all channels. Channels are organized into groups of eight and each channel group is managed by a Data Server Element (DSE). The following list gives the features of channels and DSEs:

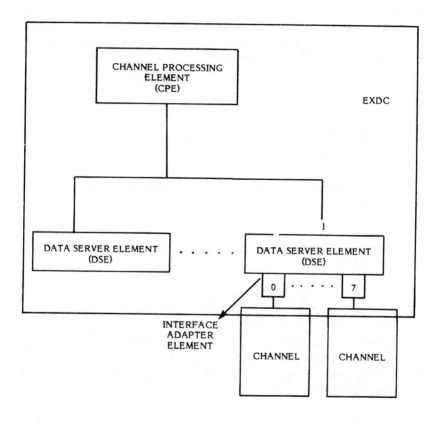

Figure 9-2/Organization of the External Data Controller
(EXDC)

o   Only byte and block multiplexer channels are supported.

o   A maximum of 24 channels (i.e., 3 channel groups of
eight channels) is supported, with a maximum of 4 byte
multiplexer channels.

o   Two channel groups is the standard feature, and one
channel group is assigned to each central processor; an
additional channel group may be optionally assigned to
either processor.

o   For each channel group, there is a Data Server Element (DSE); a channel is connected to a part in the
DSE by means of an Interface Adapter Element (IAE).

The organization of the EXDC is illustrated schematically
in Figure 9-2.   The Channel Processing Element (CPE) of
the EXDC interacts with DSEs which in turn interact with
channels.   The fetching of CCWs, analysis of status, and
presentation of interruptions is done by the CPE.   The DSE
controls channels after accepting commands from the CPE
and is responsible for data transfer between a device and
central storage.

9.4 SYSTEM CONTROLLER

This component acts as a switchboard for handling requests
between the central processors, external data processor,
and central storage.   It also acts as the arbitrator in honor-
ing storage requests that can cause contention.

9.5 COMPARISON WITH THE 3033

The 3081 processor performance is approximately equivalent to that of a tightly-coupled 3033 multiprocessing
system.   The processor cycle time of the 3081 is 26 nanoseconds as compared to 57 nanoseconds for the 3033.   The
cache size of the 3081 is 32 K as compared with 64 K for
the 3033.   The 3081 can have 24 channels as compared to
16 channels for the 3033 uniprocessor and 32 channels for a
3033 multiprocessing configuration.

Reference Material and Further Reading

o   IBM 3300 Implementation, IBM Manuals

2.1   A Guide to the IBM 3033 Processor Complex, Attached Complex, Attached Processor Complex and Multiprocessor Complex of System 370 (GC 20-1859-5)

2.2   IBM   3033   Functional   Characteristics (GA 22-7060-5)

2.3   "The IBM 3033: An Inside Look," by William D. Connors, John H. Florkowski and Samuel K. Patton, DATAMATION, May 1979.

o   IBM 370/168 Implementation, IBM Manuals

2.4   IBM System/370 Model 168 Functional Characteristics, GA 22-7010-6

2.5   A Guide to the IBM System/370 Model 168 for System/360 Users, GC 20-1787-1

o   IBM 3081 Implementation

3.5   IBM   3081   Functional   Characteristics, GA 22-7076-0

PART III
CONTROL UNIT
AND DEVICE IMPLEMENTATION

10. Concepts Used in Implementation of Control Units and Devices

In the remaining chapters we shall discuss the implementation of control units and devices. Our discussion shall be confined to two major categories of control units and devices, namely (1) those pertaining to online communication systems and (2) those pertaining to disk storage systems. But before discussion of these devices and control units, we shall present certain key concepts used in implementation.

The architecture specifies three I/O system components: channel, control unit and device. Data flow as well as control flow takes place between channel and control unit and device and control unit, the ultimate objective being the transfer of data between device and main storage. Data is transferred one byte at a time (except in the case of a two byte interface) between channel and control unit and usually on a bit-by-bit basis between device and control unit (see Figure 10-1).

10.1 SHARED AND NON-SHARED CONFIGURATIONS

There are two possible channel/control unit/device configurations. The first configuration gives rise to a tree-structure, as shown in Figure 10-2 (a). A channel is connected to several control units (no control unit is connected to more than one channel), and a control unit is connected to several devices (no device is connected to more than one control unit). The second configuration gives rise to a network structure, as shown in Figure 10-2 (b). A channel is connected to several control units (a control unit is also connected to more than one channel), and a control unit is connected to several devices (a device is also connected to more than one control unit). We shall call the first configuration a non-shared configuration because two or more channels cannot share a control unit and two or more control units cannot share a device; it is

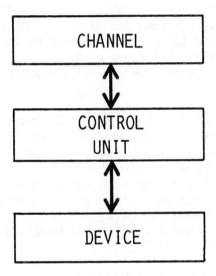

Figure 10-1/Architectural I/O Components

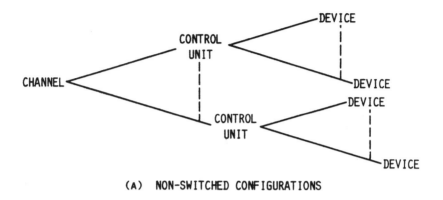

(A)   NON-SWITCHED CONFIGURATIONS

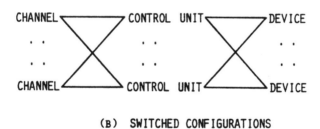

(B)   SWITCHED CONFIGURATIONS

Figure 10-2/Channel/Control Unit/Device Configurations

also called a non-switched configuration because the control units and devices do not have a hardware switch that permits such sharing. The second configuration is called a shared configuration because it permits two or more channels to share a control unit and two or more control units to share a device; it is also called a switched configuration because the control units and devices have a switch that permits such sharing.

The idea behind shared configurations is that they provide multiple I/O paths to a device from one or more processors. A set of physical channels that provide paths to a device is called a logical channel (see Figure 10-3). A uniprocessor, for example, can have logical channels having more than one member channel if the sharing capability is installed. In the case of multiprocessors, devices and control units can be shared by channel sets belonging to each CPU if such sharing capability is available. Examples of shared control units and shared devices are given in later sections.

10.2 INTERFACE BETWEEN CHANNEL AND CONTROL UNITS

A channel is connected to a maximum of eight control units via an interface which consists of parallel signal lines. Of the 48 lines available, those used for transmission of signals as shown in Figure 10-4. Figure 10-5 shows the lines that are used for control unit selection and functions related to data transfer. The lines are grouped under the following categories:

o   Tag lines (in-bound and out-bound)

o   Bus lines (in-bound and out-bound)

o   Scan Controls

o   Interlocks

o   Special Controls

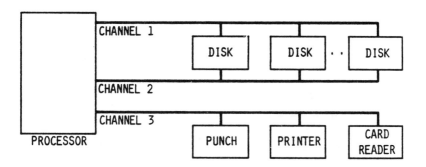

NOTES:

o   There are 3 physical channels

o   There are 2 logical channels, namely:

   -   Channels 1 and 2

   -   Channel 3

Figure 10-3/Logical Channels

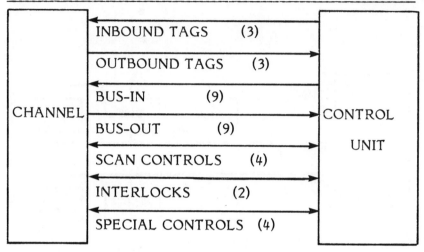

NOTES:

1. Bus lines are used for transmission of data, I/O device address, channel commands, status and sense data. Bus-in transfers data to channel and bus-out transfers data to control unit.
    Bus lines carry one byte of information plus a parity bit.
2. Tag lines identify the type of information (e.g., address, data, command) carried by the bus line.
3. Scan controls are used for polling and selection of control units.
4. Interlocks are used to ensure that only one control unit is communicating with the channel at any given time.
5. Special controls are used for metering time and other control purposes.

Figure 10-4/Interface Between Channel and Control Unit

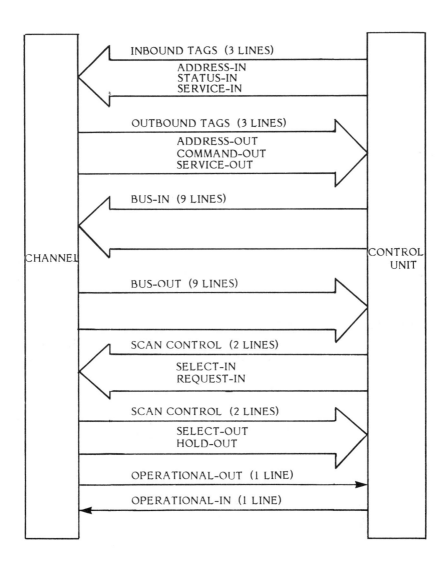

Figure 10-5/Lines Within the Interface

The bus-in and bus-out lines transfer a byte unidirectionally; actually 8 bits plus an odd parity bit (which is set to one if the byte contains an even number of one bits) are transferred. The tag lines specify the nature of the information carried by the bus lines. For example, a bus-out line may be carrying an address byte or a command byte and this is indicated by raising the address-out line or command-out line. The bus lines, in general, are used to carry the following type of information:

o Commands from CCWs

o Status

o Address

o Data

A tag line is always raised to specify the type of information contained in the bus lines.

The scan control lines are used for carrying signals to poll or select control units. By polling is meant a request to send data and by selection a command to receive data. The use of select and hold lines in this context is explained subsequently.

The interlock lines are used for locking the channel to a control unit during exchange of information. The operational-in and operational-out lines are used for this purpose, as detailed later.

The special control lines are used for metering the usage of the control units and are not used for data transfer related operations.

10.3   BASIC   PRINCIPLES   OF   CONTROL   UNIT
OPERATION

We shall recapitulate the basic principles of I/O operations outlined in the architecture. The CPU initiates an I/O operation by one of the following instructions:

o Start I/O: This instruction initiates an I/O operation that involves device control and subsequent data transfer. A channel program comprising a set of chained channel command words (CCWs) is executed by the channel and the CPU is free to execute other instructions after the channel presents initial status in the Channel Status Word (CSW). At the completion of the I/O operation (i.e., after executing the last CCW in the channel program) the channel presents an ending status in the CSW, and the CPU is interrupted by means of an I/O interruption.

o Start I/O Fast Release: This instruction initiates an I/O operation also and is similar to the Start I/O operation. The difference between Start I/O Fast Release (SIOF) and Start I/O (SIO) is that the SIOF is executed if the channel is available and the SIO is executed if channel, control unit, and device are available. In the case of SIO, the CPU is free to execute the next instruction only after the device is selected, assuming that channel, control unit and device are available. In the case of SIOF, the instruction is executed without waiting for device selection and a deferred condition code is set in the CSW if the control unit or device is not available. SIOF is used usually with block multiplexer channels connected to disk drives.

The CPU issues the Test I/O and Clear I/O instructions for testing and sensing status of channel, device, and control unit. Halt I/O and the Halt Device instructions are used for discontinuing I/O operations.

The various phases of control unit operation are the following:

o Initial selection of a control unit by the channel

o Service request to a channel by a control unit and reselection by the channel o   Data transfer

o   Ending sequence

We shall discuss next each of these phases in some detail.

Initial Selection. Control units are connected to the interface in a priority sequence. The channel selects a specified control unit by sending a device address to all control units connected to it.

The channel sends an address byte on the bus-out line and raises address-out, select out, and hold-out lines. The first control unit compares the address on the bus line with addresses of devices attached to it and upon an equal comparison indicates that (1) it is busy, by sending a status byte via the bus-in line and raising the status-in line or (2) it is available, by raising the operational-in line and sending the device address via the bus-in line. Assuming that the control unit is available, the channel transmits a command byte via bus-out and the control unit responds with an initial status byte (which is zero if the device is not busy) and the channel acknowledges by raising the service-out line. The initial selection phase is completed at the end of this signal. Figure 10-6 illustrates the sequence of events described so far.

If the first control unit finds that the address comparison does not result in a match, it propagates the select-out signal to the second control unit which performs an address comparison. A priority scheme obtained as a result of wiring and select-out and select-in line determines what control unit is first, second and so forth. The select-out line returns to the channel and becomes the select-in line as shown in Figure 10-7. Notice the difference between the select lines and other lines as shown in Figure 10-7. The channel drives all other out lines but the select-out line is driven by one control unit to the next in sequence of priority.

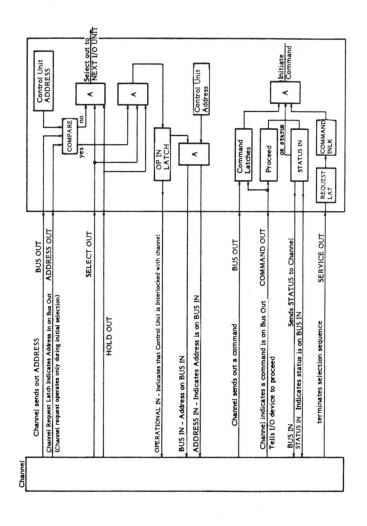

Figure 10-6/Initial Selection Sequence

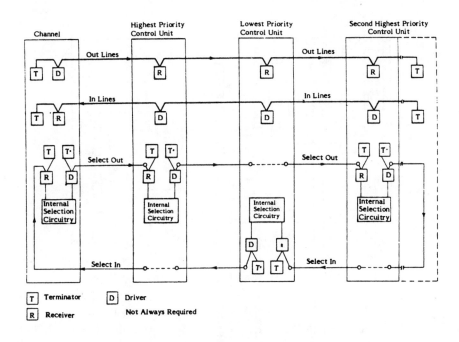

Figure 10-7/Arrangement of Control Units on Select-in and
Select-out Lines

To summarize, during the initial selection phase the channel takes the initiative by raising the address-out line, placing the address of the device on the bus-out line, and raising select-out. The select-out signal is blocked by a control unit during address comparison and is subsequently propagated to the next control unit in priority sequence until an address equal comparison occurs when the operational-in line is raised by the control unit and the channel is locked in to the control unit. The channel then sends a command (from the first CCW of the channel program) to the control unit, and the control unit responds with an initial status byte to the channel.

Service Request by the Control Unit and Reselection. After initial selection, the control unit decodes the command it has received and sends it to the device for execution. During the time necessary for the execution of the command, the channel is not locked-in to the control unit (unless it is a selector channel). When the device operation is complete, the control unit notifies the channel that it requires service by raising the request-in line. The channel responds by raising select-out and hold-out lines. The select-out signal is propagated from control unit to control unit in priority sequence until it reaches the one that raised the request line. This control unit places its address on the bus-in line and interlocks the channel by raising the operational-in line. The channel responds by raising the command-out line, in effect asking the control unit to go ahead with data transfer.

Data Transfer. The control unit places a data byte on the bus-in and raises the service-in line for transfer to the channel (resulting from a read operation). For transfer of data to the control unit from the channel (resulting from a write operation), the control unit raises the service-in line and the channel responds by placing a data byte on bus-out and raising the service-out line.

There are two modes of data transfer: byte multiplex

mode and burst mode. In the byte multiplex mode, after one byte of data is transferred the connection between channel and control unit is ended by the fall of the operational-in interlock line. In the burst mode, a string of bytes is transferred one byte at a time and the operational-in interlock line is held for the duration of the transfer. The rule of thumb is that if the operational-in interlock line is held for less than 32 microseconds byte multiplex mode is assumed; if the line is held for more than 32 microseconds, the transfer is considered to be in the burst mode.

Ending Sequence: In situations where an I/O device recognizes the end of an operation before or simultaneously with the channel, the control unit places a status byte on bus-in and raises the status-in line.

When the channel wants to end an I/O operation before the I/O device has indicated completion, the channel sends a stop signal (by raising the command-out line) to the control unit when it asks for channel service. The control unit continues to function until the end of the operation without asking for channel service and sends a status byte at that time.

11. Control Units and Devices Used in Communication Networks

Before describing control units and devices used in communication, it is necessary to give a presentation of the fundamental concepts used in IBM communication networks. The hardware components of an IBM communication network are the following:

o Host(s)

o Communication Controllers

o Cluster Controllers

o Terminals

o Data Links

o Modems

There are two ways of attaching a communications controller to a host, namely, (1) directly to the channel (called local attachment) and (2) to another communications controller via communication lines and modem (called remote attachment). Also, there are two ways of attaching a terminal to a host, namely (1) directly to the channel via the terminal's control unit (called local attachment) and (2) to a local or remote communications controller via communications line and modem (called remote attachment).

A communications controller attached to a channel (local attachment) is viewed as a control unit as defined in the 370 architecture. A byte multiplexer or block multiplexer channel is used for this purpose, and the rules of initial selection, reselection, data transfer and ending sequence described previously are followed. A terminal connected to a channel via the terminal's own control unit (local attachment) is regarded as a device as defined in the 370 architecture.

The 370 architecture, however, does not make specifications regarding remote attachments and leaves it as a matter of implementation. The IBM network architecture for communication networks using remote and local attachments is known as Systems Network Architecture (SNA) and it presents the hardware and software functional requirements for the various components of a network. The current implementation of SNA is done by means of the Advanced Communication Function (ACF) software which provides the following support:

o   A network Control Program (NCP) for the IBM 3705

o   Data Communication Software for the Host (IMS, CICS)

o   Communication Access Methods for the Host (VTAM, TCAM)

o   Communication Protocols (BSC, SDLC, start-stop)

We shall not go into details of the software aspects of communication networks and the interested reader can consult references given at the end of this chapter.

A general schematic of a communication network running under a single host using ACF/VTAM is given in Figure 11-1. The communications controllers are connected directly to a host channel (called local attachment) or to another communications controller (called remote attachment) via communication lines. Terminals can be attached locally to the host channel or to the communications controller via communication lines. The IBM 3270 and IBM 3790 are commonly used terminals. A general schematic of a communication network using multiple hosts is given in Figure 11-2. The word domain is used to collectively denote the host, locally attached communications controller, and remote attachments that are part of the local communications controller. Networking between

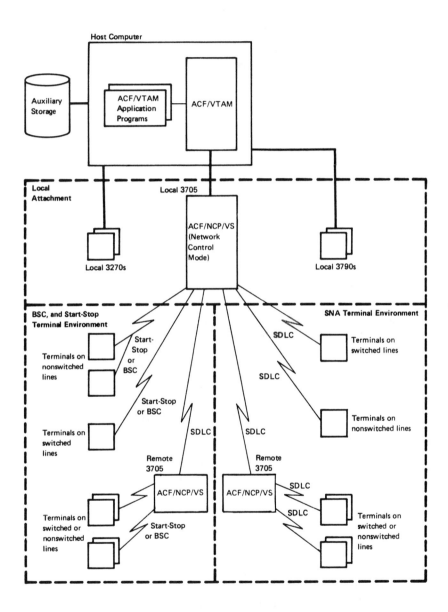

Figure 11-1/Communication Network Under SNA
(Single Host)

multiple hosts is viewed as a cross-domain activity. In Figure 11-3, a frequently used banking application network is shown. The IBM 3600 Finance Communication System can support bank teller operations and Automatic Teller Machines (ATMs). The system consists of a controller that supports terminals and printers that are connected in a loop. The host has a library of IBM 3600 application programs, created by the Subsystem Support Service (SSS), which are a set of service programs supplied by IBM. The 3600 uses these application programs (written in the 3600 assembler language) for performing arithmetic, logical and transmission functions. The arithmetic and logical functions can be used to do totals required by bank tellers and similar functions. In the host, IMS or CICS application programs can access the 3600 units using call functions that are provided by IMS or CICS. For details regarding the 3600, see reference 3.16. Another example of a network is the distributed word processing network shown in Figure 11-4, where IBM 8100 minicomputers running under the Distributed Processing Control Executive (DPCX) are connected to host computers. Several capabilities are provided by the host in document processing, such as the document facility library (DLF) which keeps a library of documents that are used by the Advanced Text Management System (ATMS), or the Document Composition Facility (DCF). The two distributed capabilities are the following:

o   The interchange of documents between host and the 8100, via the Document Interchange Facility.

o   The central storage of documents and the use of a document data base at the host, via the Distributed Office Support System.

At the 8100 level, the capability for text entry and display via IBM 3730 terminals is provided by the Distributed Office Support Facility (DOSF) which also contains a Document Transmission Function (DTF) for transmission to the host. IMS, CICS, or VTAM perform archival and retrieval functions. For details regarding the system, see reference 3.15.

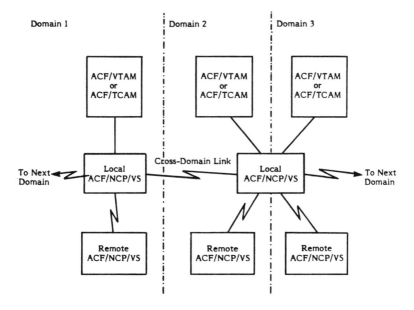

Figure 11-2/Multi-Host Communication Network Using
Shared 3705 Under SNA

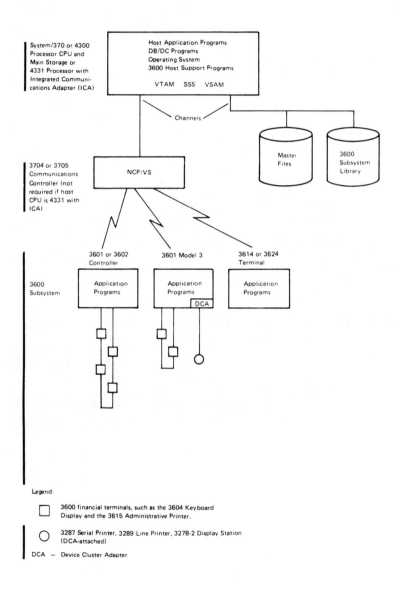

Figure 11-3/3600 Finance Communication System Under SNA

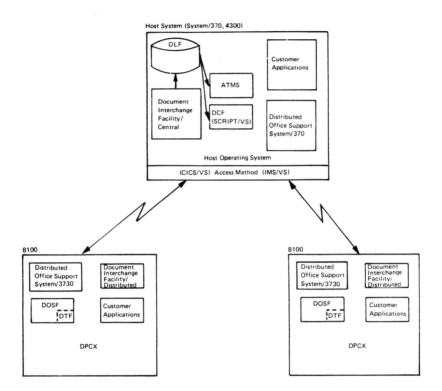

Figure 1. System Relationships in a Sample Network

Figure 11-4/Distributed Word Processing System

The basic hardware components of these networks are, as mentioned before, hosts, communication controllers and terminals. The terminals may be connected directly to the host via a channel, or to a communications controller via modems and data links. Terminals may also be connected to a cluster controller (e.g., the IBM 3601 Finance Communication Controller or the IBM 8100 minicomputer in a document processing network) which, in turn, is attached to a host channel or to the communications controller.

In this chapter we shall be concerned with the functions of the communications controller and IBM terminals. In order to explain these functions properly, we shall present next certain introductory concepts in data communication.

11.1 FUNDAMENTALS OF IBM DATA COMMUNICATION

Start/Stop Terminals. IBM uses two types of terminals called start/stop (also known as asynchronous) terminals and synchronous terminals. Start/Stop terminals transmit data on a character-by-character basis, and each character is framed by a start bit and a stop bit. The start bit (also called a space) is a zero bit and the stop bit (also called a mark) is a one-bit. Figure 11-5 illustrates the framing of a character by start/stop bits. The characters are transmitted randomly, and a series of one bits (called mark hold) are used to fill up the space between non-contiguous characters.

The following general rules apply to asynchronous transmission:

-       The line is kept in the one-state (i.e., the state corresponding to mark hold) when no data is being sent.

-       When the line goes from the one-state to the zero-state (i.e., the state corresponding to the start bit) the receiver activates a clock which is used for sampling other bits as they are transmitted down the line.

- The receiver keeps track of the number of bits
that constitute a character and when all character bits have been received, it resynchronizes
itself with the transmitter.

Several IBM start/stop devices use a simple protocol,
derived from the following special characters:

EOB -- End of Block character, to indicate the
end of a data block.

EOT -- End of Transmission, to indicate the end
of a message comprising several blocks.

EOA -- End of Address, to indicate the end of
terminal address or the beginning of data.

SOA -- Start of Address, to indicate the beginning of a terminal address.

Negative Response -- To indicate that data was
not received correctly.

Positive Response -- To indicate that data was
received correctly.

These special control characters are placed before,
after or between text characters and the receiver
decodes them and takes appropriate action.

<u>Synchronous Terminals.</u> Unlike start/stop terminals,
synchronous terminals transmit and receive data
without the framing bits to indicate the beginning and
ending of each character. Synchronous terminals are
buffered terminals; the contents of the buffer are
transmitted serially on a bit-by-bit basis. The time
interval between each bit is constant and is controlled
by a clock within the terminal. The receiving terminal
has a clock also, and synchronization between the two
clocks is achieved by means of the duration of bit
patterns that are recognized by both parties as syn-

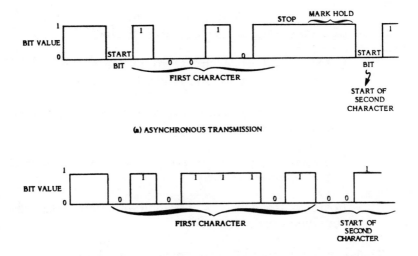

(a) ASYNCHRONOUS TRANSMISSION

(b) SYNCHRONOUS TRANSMISSION

Figure 11-5/ Character Framing by Start/Stop Bits

chronizing signals.

IBM uses two protocols for synchronous communication, namely binary synchronous communication (BSC) and Synchronous Data Link Control (SDLC). BSC was developed in the early sixties to support the EBCDIC code used by the IBM 360 and is supported by the Basic Telecommunications Access Method (BTAM). SDLC is a more recent protocol and is supported by the later access methods such as Virtual Telecommunication Access Method (VTAM).

Lines, Modems and Interfaces. A terminal or a computer transmitting or receiving data either synchronously or asynchronously via communication lines has to interface with a modem at both ends of the transmission (see Figure 11-6). A modem (Modulator DeModulator) is a data communication device that transforms binary signals (i.e., zeroes or ones) from a terminal or a computer to an analog waveform which is sent over communication lines; it also performs the reverse operation, namely convert an analog waveform into binary signals. There is a wide variety of modems available in the market, offering a wide range of transmission speeds and capabilities to interface with synchronous or asynchronous terminals.

A terminal (or a computer) is connected to a modem by means of a standard interface. Two of the commonly used standard interfaces are the following:

-    Electronic Industries Association's (EIA) RS 232C.

-    International Telegraph & Telephone Consultative Committee's (CCITT) V24.

These interfaces arose from standardization of the interconnection between data terminal equipment (DTE) and data communication equipment (DCE). The RS 232C interface is a 25 pin connector that specifies

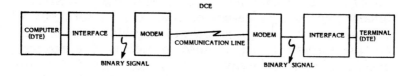

Figure 11-6/Data Links

pin assignments for sending and receiving signals. Figure 11-7 shows the pin connections to be made to the terminal and to the modem and the function of each circuit.

A communication line that can transmit and receive at the same time is called full duplex; a communication line that permits transmission or reception, but not both simultaneously, is called a half-duplex line. In the case of a half-duplex line, the line has to be "turned around" for transmission after it has been used for reception and vice versa. There is a finite time interval (e.g., 50 to 250 milliseconds, depending on distance) associated with line turn-around; this time is required for reversing the direction of echo suppressors in the telephone line (an echo suppressor is a device for attenuating the echo and improving the quality of the line) and for allowing modems to stabilize.

A communication line can be permanently connected between a terminal and a computer, in which case it is called leased or non-switched. In such a case, no dialing is necessary on the part of the sender or the receiver. Alternately, a terminal can be connected to a computer via a dial-up line (also known as a switched line) whereby the sender dials a telephone number for establishing connection. Assuming that the sender is using a terminal, the modem at the computer should be able to answer the incoming call and then enter a data mode. An example of such a modem is the Bell System 103A, which is connected to the computer as well as to an auxiliary telephone. An AUTO push button allows the modem to automatically accept the telephone call from the terminal and to enter into the data communication mode. The computer needs an Automatic Calling Unit if it is to dial a number automatically in order to send a message.

Point-to-Point and Multipoint Configurations. We shall use the word station to denote a device that can perform data transmission and reception (e.g., termin

INTERCHANGE CIRCUIT	CCITT V24 EQUIVALENT	DESCRIPTION	GND	DATA		CONTROL		TIMING	
				FROM DCE	TO DCE	FROM DCE	TO DCE	FROM DCE	TO DCE
AA	101	Protective Ground	X						
AB	102	Signal Ground/Common Return	X						
BA	103	Transmitted Data			X				
BB	104	Received Data		X					
CA	105	Request to Send					X		
CB	106	Clear to Send				X			
CC	107	Data Set Ready				X			
CD	108.2	Data Terminal Ready					X		
CE	125	Ring Indicator				X			
CF	109	Received Line Signal Detector				X			
CG	110	Signal Quality Detector				X			
CH	111	Data Signal Rate Selector (DTE)					X		
CI	112	Data Signal Rate Selector (DCE)				X			
DA	113	Transmitter Signal Element Timing (DTE)							X
DB	114	Transmitter Signal Element Timing (DCE)						X	
DD	115	Receiver Signal Element Timing (DCE)						X	
SBA	118	Secondary Transmitted Data			X				
SBB	119	Secondary Received Data		X					
SCA	120	Secondary Request to Send					X		
SCB	121	Secondary Clear to Send				X			
SCF	122	Secondary Received Line Signal Detector				X			

EIA RS232C Interface Connector Pin Assignments

Pin Number	Circuit	Description
1	AA	Protective Ground
2	BA	Transmitted Data
3	BB	Received Data
4	CA	Request to Send
5	CB	Clear to Send
6	CC	Data Set Ready
7	AB	Signal Ground (Common Return)
8	CF	Received Line Signal Detector
9	—	(Reserved for Data Testing)
10	—	(Reserved for Data Set Testing)
11	—	Unassigned
12	SCF	Secondary Received Line Signal Detector
13	SCB	Secondary Clear to Send
14	SBA	Secondary Transmitted Data
15	DB	Transmission Signal Element Timing (DCE Source)
16	SBB	Secondary Received Data
17	DD	Receiver Signal Element Timing (DCE Source)
18		Unassigned
19	SCA	Secondary Request to Send
20	CD	Data Terminal Ready
21	CG	Signal Quality Detector
22	CE	Ring Indicator
23	CH/CI	Data Signal Rate Selector (DTE/DCE Source)
24	DA	Transmit Signal Element Timing (DTE Source)
25		Unassigned

Figure 11-7/RS 232C Interface Specification

al, computer). A point-to-point configuration is a connection between two stations such that a communication line is used exclusively by the two stations. In a point-to-point configuration, one station is called a primary (also known as master) and the other station is called a secondary (also known as slave). Either station can bid for the use of the line in transmitting messages. When it is not transmitting, a station monitors the line for control characters indicating message transmission by the other station and "times out" if no control characters are monitored within a definite time interval. If both stations bid at the same time, the contention is resolved in favor of the primary. In actual practice, what happens is that both stations go from the transmitting into the monitoring mode, and the station with the shorter time-out comes out of the monitoring mode and starts sending data; the station with the shorter time out is the primary station. In contrast to the point-to-point configuration, a multipoint (or multidropped) configuration allows a line to be used by several stations. In a multipoint configuration, one station (usually the computer) is called the control station and the other stations are called tributaries. The control station solicits data to send from each tributary station that is multidropped on the line. This invitation to send data is known as a polling operation. When the control station has data to send, it notifies the appropriate tributary by means of an operation known as selection.

Binary Synchronous Communication (BSC). IBM introduced BSC in 1966 and it is still widely used by many computer and terminal manufacturers as a communications protocol. BSC is easy to implement and to understand and there is little doubt that it will be in use for a number of years.

The main characteristics of BSC are the following:

-   It is primarily designed for half-duplex lines and the protocol follows the conventions of a dialogue.

- It is applicable to synchronous stations connected in a point-to-point or multipoint configuration.

- It adds control characters to data characters in order to conduct the dialog and also to perform synchronization functions.

- Messages are transmitted in blocks and each byte within a block is sent without start/stop bits; a block is thus a sequence of bits sent at regular intervals.

The sending and receiving modems should be in synchronization in order to transmit successfully a message block. BSC provides for synchronization at a bit level and character level.

Two stations achieve bit synchronization under BSC by means of a special synchronization character (called PAD) which is inserted into the beginning of the text. The bit configuration of the PAD character (alternating zeros and ones) can be used by the receiver to synchronize its clock with that of the sender at the beginning of a transmission sequence. In addition, BSC provides for character synchronization by means of a special character called SYN (whose bit configuration is 01100010) which is usually inserted into the message text at periodic intervals. After a line turnaround, the sequence PAD SYN SYN is sent prior to messages in BSC format in order to achieve synchronization between the two modems at bit and character levels.

In BSC, a message is divided into blocks. The first block consists of an optional header and text data. The succeeding blocks contain only text data. control characters are used for identifying header and text, and also for the end of a block or a message. Typically, a message will have the following appearance:

SOH header STX text ETB text ETB..... text ETX, where SOH, STX, ETB, ETX denote the start of a header, start of text, end of a text block and end of text.

In a point-to-point configuration, the primary station (or control station) conducts a BSC session by using the following procedure:

1) Inquiry -- The primary station transmits a control character called ENQ.

2) Negative response to the inquiry -- If the secondary has no messages to send, it transmits a control character called EOT (End of Transmission).

3) Positive response to the inquiry -- If the secondary has a message to send, it transmits a message in blocks.

4) Affirmative acknowledgement of a block -- The primary or control station acknowledges the receipt of each message block by alternately sending an ACK0 or ACK1 character; ACK0 is sent for the first acknowledgement, ACK1 for the second, ACK0 for the third, ACK1 for the fourth and so on.

5) Negative acknowledgement of a block -- The primary station sends a negative acknowledgement control character (NAK) in case a block is received incorrectly.

6) End of transmission -- When all blocks comprising the message have been transmitted, the sender transmits an EOT to indicate the end of transmission.

In the case of multipoint configuration, each tributary station is polled by the control station to send data. Each tributary station has a unique polling address, and the control station sends the address of the station followed by ENQ down the line. Each tributary station monitors the line and compares the address with its own; if a match occurs, it responds with one of the following:

1)   EOT -- The tributary has nothing to send.

2)   STX ENQ -- The tributary has temporary text delay and it cannot send data within the next few seconds.

3)   SOH header STX text ETX -- The tributary sends a message in BSC format to the control station.

In the first two cases, the control station polls the next tributary, and if it has nothing to send, the next tributary is polled and so forth. The order of polling is determined by means of a polling list which contains an ordered sequence of tributary addresses. In the last case, the control station receives the first message block, acknowledges with an ACK0, and the tributary sends the next block which is acknowledged with an ACK1 and so forth until the tributary indicates end of transmission by sending EOT. During the transmission of the message, the control station does not poll any other station multidropped from the line.

When the control station has a message to send to a tributary, it "selects" the tributary by sending the address of the tributary followed by an ENQ down the line. Note that each tributary has two unique addresses, one for polling and one for selection. Each tributary compares the selection address with its own, and on an equal comparison comes up with one of the following responses:

1)   ACK0 -- The tributary is prepared to receive.

2)   NAK -- The tributary is not prepared to receive.

In the first case, the control station sends its message and the tributary uses an alternating ACK1/ACK0 sequence to acknowledge the transmission of each block. In the second case, the control station tries again after a predetermined interval, and if selection is not completed after a predetermined number of trials, an error condition is generated.

We shall describe next the function of an important control character used in BSC called Data Link Escape (DLE), which is used for "transparent" BSC transmission. In certain situations (e.g., when transmitting program load modules) the text may contain bit configurations pertaining to control characters like SOH, ENQ, etc. In such a situation, a DLE character is inserted before every control character in the text (e.g., SOH becomes DLE SOH, STX becomes DLE STX, and the occurrence of a DLE gives rise to DLE DLE). This mode of operation is called transparent, since control characters can also become part of the text.

Synchronous Data Link Control (SDLC). SDLC is IBM's new data link protocol and it has many features which make it more efficient than BSC. Its main characteristics are given below:

- SDLC is designed for operation with full-duplex lines (it can be used with half-duplex lines also) and can be used with point-to-point and multipoint configurations.

- SDLC uses the concept of a primary station and secondary stations in both point-to-point and multipoint configurations; the primary station initiates transmission activity by polling the secondary station(s).

- A primary station can set a secondary station in one of three modes:

  o   Normal Response Mode (NRM) in which the secondary station transmits data when it is polled by the primary. (Note that the primary polls each secondary in turn and after it issues a poll to a secondary, it waits for an answer before issuing a poll to another secondary.)

o   Initialization Mode, in which the primary
    sends a command to initialize the second-
    ary; initialization procedures vary accord-
    ing to the type of terminal.

o   Normal Disconnected Mode (NDM) in which
    the secondary is off-line and responds to
    mode setting commands from the primary;
    on receiving a polling command, the sec-
    ondary makes a request to be initialized.

-   The basic SDLC message unit is called a frame; a
    uniquely encoded flag byte (with a bit configura-
    tion 01111110) indicates the start of a frame.

-   When a string of five one bits is encountered by
    the sender in a context other than in a flag field,
    a zero bit is automatically inserted (this proce-
    dure is called bit-stuffing) and the receiver
    deletes the zero bit if it is preceded by five one
    bits; this procedure is necessary to make the six
    one bit string configuration in the flag field a
    unique occurrence.

-   SDLC achieves synchronization by a technique
    called Non-Return-to-Zero-Inverted (NRZI) under
    which the binary signal from the sender changes
    state when the next bit to be transmitted is a
    zero and does not change state when the next bit
    to be transmitted is a one; notice that since bit-
    stuffing is used, there can be at most a string of
    six one bits (corresponding to the flag byte) and
    hence the line will be in any one state for a
    maximum duration of six bits.

We shall next outline the method of operation employed by SDLC. Figure 11-8 shows the structure of
SDLC frames. There are three types of SDLC frames,
namely:

o   Information Transfer

o   Supervisory

o   Nonsequenced

The information transfer frame (I frame) is used for transmission of message text and is identified by a 0 in bit position zero of the control field (see Figure 11-8). Each frame is numbered from zero through seven and separate sequence numbers are kept for sent and received frames. In Figure 11-8, Ns and Nr indicate the count of frames sent and frames received. The count wraps around after seven and automatically becomes zero. The P/F bit is used both by primary and secondary. When used by the primary, the on condition of the bit indicates that the primary is asking the secondary to confirm the number of frames it has received via the receive sequence field Ns and is called the Poll bit. When used by the secondary, the bit is called the Final bit and when it is on, the secondary confirms the number of frames that it has received via the Ns field.

The supervisory format frame is indicated by the bit configuration 10 for the two leading bits in the control field. The supervisory format is used for sending up to four commands (indicated by SS in Figure 11-8). Only three such commands are actually used in SDLC and they are the following:

RR   --   "Receive Ready" is used when the receiver is ready to accept I frames and also to acknowledge I frames already received.

RNR -- "Receive not ready" indicates that the receiver is temporarily busy and also to acknowledge frames received up to that point.

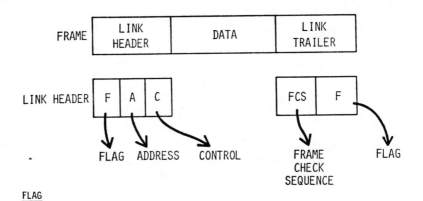

FLAG

- FLAG has unique 8 bit sequence - 0 1 1 1 1 1 1 0

  6 bits

CONTROL

SENT FIRST

CONTROL FIELD BITS

FRAME TYPE	0	1	2	3	4	5	6	7
INFORMATION TRANSFER FORMAT	0	Ns			P/F	Nr		
SUPERVISORY FORMAT	1	0	S	S	P/F	Nr		
NONSEQUENCED FORMAT	1	1	M	M	P/F	M	M	M

Explanation: Ns and Nr denote send and receive sequence numbers.

SS, MM and MMM denote command bits.

P/F denotes Poll/Final Bit

Figure 11-8/ SDLC Frame Structure

REJ --   "Reject" indicates that frames starting with a certain sequence number have been rejected by the receiver and to request retransmission.

The Nonsequenced format is indicated by two leading one bits in the control field. The format is used for issuing commands (up to 32 commands are available corresponding to the five M bits as shown in Figure 11-8) and some of the commands are described below:

o   Set Normal Response Mode (SNRM) -- This command puts the secondary in the Normal Response mode; the secondary cannot transmit unless the primary solicits such transmission with the poll bit on. The SNRM command itself must have the poll bit turned on, and the secondary acknowledges the command by responding with Nonsequenced Acknowledge (NSA) with the F-bit on.

o   Nonsequenced Acknowledge (NSA) -- This response is elicited by the SNRM command.

o   Request Initialization (RQI) -- This request is issued by the secondary station to initialize it so that it becomes fully operational; such initialization can be performed by an initial program load (IPL) or initial microcode load (IML).

o   Set Initialization Mode (SIM) -- This command is issued after an RQI is received by the primary station and it initiates IPL or IML functions required to make the secondary fully operational.

An example of SDLC multipoint operation over a full duplex line is given in Figure 11-9. There are two secondary stations denoted by B and n. B is in normal disabled mode (NDM) and n is in normal response mode (NRM). The notation used in Figure 11-9 needs explanation. A transmission sequence contains the address of the secondary, the mnemonic for the command or response, the Ns and Nr count, and the P/F bit setting. In Figure 11-9, the following conventions are observed:

o   A hyphen indicates that the Ns count is not required.

o   A P or F indicates that the poll or final bit is on.

o   A bar over P or F indicates that the poll or final bit is off.

o   A number enclosed in parentheses is the Ns count or the Nr count; in the case of an I frame the first number is the Ns count and the second is the Nr count. In the case of an RR frame only the Nr count is given.

The notation B, RR - P (0) means that a supervisory frame with RR command is sent without an Ns, with the poll bit on and with the Nr count set to zero. In Figure 11-9, the primary polls B for status and sets it in NRM mode by sending RR, SIM and SNRM commands. It sends next two information frames number 0 and 1 and then asks for confirmation by sending B, RR - P (0). B confirms sending B, RR - F (2), which indicates that the Final bit is on and the Nr count is 2; it should be noted that the Nr count is one higher than the Ns of the last received frame. A then sends B three more frames and B confirms by sending B; RR - F (5).

11.2 IBM 3705 COMMUNICATIONS CONTROLLER

The IBM 3705 is a commonly used communications controller. It is a special purpose minicomputer having a CPU, main storage, and specialized communication hardware. It does not support peripheral units like disks, tapes or printers nor does it support high level programming languages or a sophisticated operating system. It has an assembly language, but programs are assembled at the host and transferred to the 3705 via the host channel.

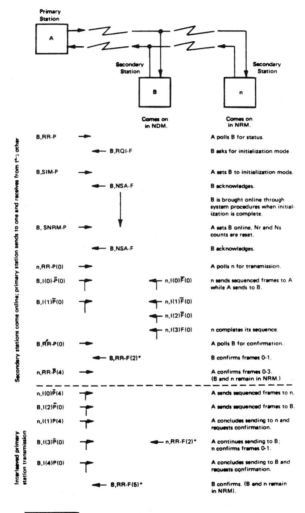

Figure 11-9/Example of SDLC Frame Exchange
(Multipoint Full Duplex)

11.2.1 Overview

The operation of the 3705 is schematically illustrated in Figure 11-10. The major components of the 3705 are the following:

o   Central Control Unit (CCU)

o   Channel Adapter

o   Main Storage

o   Communications Scanner

The Central Control Unit functions as a CPU with registers, interruption capability, and an instruction set. The CCU fetches instructions from the 3705 main storage and executes them like any other computer.

The channel adapter is attached to the host channel and its function is to act as the intermediary in data transfer between channel and CCU or channel and main storage of the 3705.

The communication scanner acts as an intermediary in data transfer between the 3705 and a communications terminal. All communication scanners are attached to the 3705 via an attachment base. A communication line is attached to the scanner via a line interface base, as illustrated in Figure 11-12.

The 3705 comes in two versions, 3705-I and 3705-II. Both versions have basic frames, and the basic frames can be enhanced incrementally by means of expansion frames. Thus, in the case of 3705-II, the following can be incrementally modified:

-    Storage (in 64K bytes)

-    Channel Adapters

-    Communication Scanners

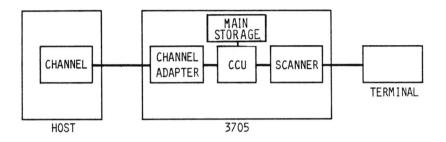

NOTES:

o   Data is transmitted between host and local 3705 via channel and channel adapter.

o   Data is transmitted between 3705 and remote terminal via communication scanner and communication lines.

o   To the host, the 3705 logically appears like a control unit and data is transmitted one byte at a time between channel and channel adapter.

Figure 11-10/Simplified Schematic Diagram Showing 3705 Operation

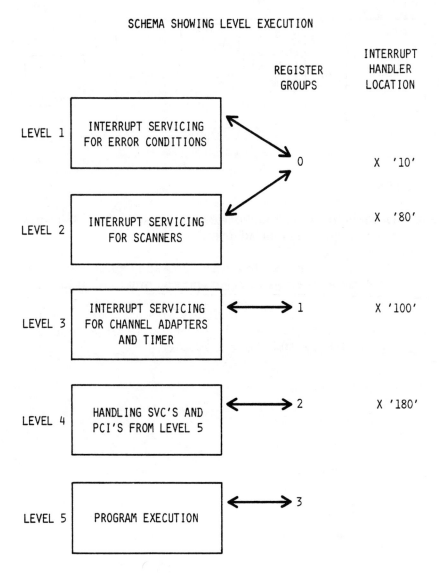

Figure 11-11/Schema Showing Level Execution

- Line Interface Bases

There are complicated restrictions on the number and types of channel adapters allowed under each incremental configuration. The reader is referred to the bibliography at the end of Part III for further references.

The 3705 operates in two modes, called the emulation mode and native mode. In the emulation mode, the 3705 emulates an IBM 270X (X = 1, 2, 3) also known as a Transmission Control Unit (TCU). The 270X can be regarded as the precursor of the 3705. The earlier communication access methods, like Basic Telecommunications Access Method (BTAM), were designed for the 270X whereas the later communication access methods, like Virtual Telecommunications Access Method (VTAM), are designed for the 3705 in its native mode.

The mode of operation for the 3705 is decided by the access method used in the host. If the host uses BTAM, an Emulation Program (EP) is loaded into the 3705 and the 3705 behaves like a 270X. If the host uses VTAM, the Network Control Program (NCP) is loaded into the 3705 and the 3705 functions in its native mode. A feature of NCP known as the Partitioned Emulation Program (PEP) enables the 3705 to function in both modes; this means that some terminals can be accessed by VTAM and the others by BTAM. The main differences between the two modes are given below:

1) In the emulation mode, the host controls the network and performs all network functions (including polling and selection); in the native mode, the network control functions are distributed between the host and the 3705 and the latter performs polling, selection and various control functions.

2) In the emulation mode, the 3705 is assigned a subchannel address for each communication line; in the native mode the 3705 is assigned only one subchannel address for all lines.

11.2.2 Component Description

We shall describe next the main components of the 3705.

Main Storage. The main storage comes in modules and ranges from 32K to 512K bytes, depending on the model that is being used. The memory cycle time is either 0.9 m.s. or 1.0 m.s. depending on the model.

The basic storage addressing scheme uses 16 bits (i.e., the address space is 64K bytes); to expand the address space beyond 64K, a feature called extended addressing is used. Up to 3 bits of an additional byte is used for increasing the size of the address space up to 512K. When the extended address capability is used, all registers in the CCU are expanded to handle up to 20 bits, and 3705 programs should be designed to handle 20 bit registers.

Central Control Unit. The Central Control Unit (CCU) is similar to a CPU. Its functions are (1) decoding of instructions, (2) performing storage operations, (3) performing arithmetic and logical operations, and (4) executing I/O instructions.

The CCU has five levels of operation, called interrupt levels. These levels are numbered from one to five in descending priority (level 1 has the highest priority and level 5 has the lowest priority).

Each level has a set of eight registers associated with it (the only exception is in the case of levels 1 and 2 which share a set of registers) and performs a specified set of functions as indicated below:

Level 1:   This level handles interrupts caused by error conditions, (e.g., CCU checks, scanner or channel adapter checks, addressing exceptions).

Level 2:   This level handles scanner interrupts, (e.g., after a scanner has finished assembling a character, it interrupts the CCU at this level).

Level 3: This level handles channel adapter interrupts.

Level 4: This level handles Supervisory Calls (SVC) and Program Controlled Interruption (PCI) requests issued by 3705 programs running at level 5.

Level 5: This level is the lowest level and cannot interrupt other levels; 3705 programs run at this level.

The interrupt handling routines for levels 1 to 4 have the following properties:

o   Interrupts are serviced on a priority basis; the servicing of an interrupt at a given priority can be interrupted by an interrupt having higher priority.

o   When an interrupt is being serviced at any given level, a "latch" is on and no interruptions at the same level are allowed until the completion of interrupt servicing.

o   When an interrupt is serviced at any given level, the interrupt servicing routine begins executing a program starting at an address at a pre-specified hardware location (e.g., level 1 is X "10", level 2 X "80", level 3 X "110", level 4 X "180").

o   After servicing the interrupt, the routine exits that level by an EXIT instruction.

o   When level 5 uses the EXIT instruction, it issues a supervisory call (SVC) at level 4.

Figure 11-11 shows a schema for level execution. In

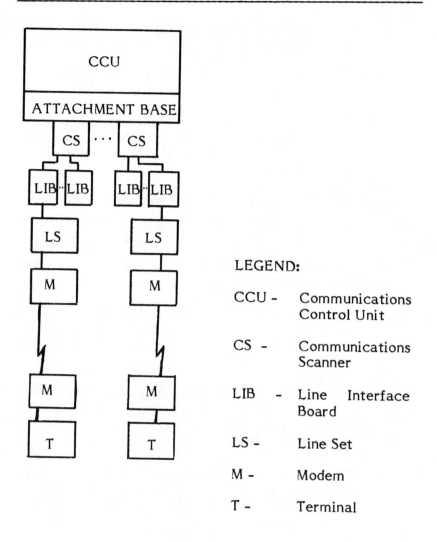

LEGEND:

CCU - Communications Control Unit

CS - Communications Scanner

LIB - Line Interface Board

LS - Line Set

M - Modem

T - Terminal

Figure 11-12/Communications Scanner Configuration

summary, the main features of the level structure in the 3705 are as follows:

o   Programs are executed at level 5.

o   Scanners and channel adapters have their own interrupt levels.

o   Interrupt levels are prioritized, with level 1 having the highest priority.

o   The EXIT instruction is used to exit from a given level.

In addition to the level registers, there is a set of external registers associated with channel adapters, scanners and CCU. The programs (executing at level 5) can manipulate these external registers to perform input/output, status sense, and control operations. Instructions involving external registers use the commands Input X "nn" or Output X "nn" where nn is a hexidecimal number associated with an external register.

The instruction set of the CCU comprise arithmetic, logical, branching, and I/O operations and also a level exit operation. The formats of non-I/O instructions are given below:

RR   -   Register to Register

RS   -   Register to Storage

RT   -   Branching Operation

RA   -   Register to Immediate Address

RSA -   Register to Storage with Addition

RE   -   Register to External Register

RI   -   Register to Immediate Operand

Typical instructions are Store Character, Add Register Immediate, Compare Register, etc. An instruction takes a maximum of 2 storage cycles (i.e., 2 m.s.) for execution.

Communication Scanners. The function of scanners is to scan communication lines, to perform assembly or disassembly of characters, to provide buffering services, and to cause interrupts. The analog data that is transmitted over communication lines is transformed by a modem into serial bits and the scanner assembles these bits into characters. There are three types of scanners called Type 1, Type 2, and Type 3. Their distinguishing characteristics are noted below.

o   Type 1 Scanner: This scanner is the least sophisticated of the three and its method of operation consists of interrupting the CCU each time a bit is received from a communication line.

o   Type 2 Scanner: This scanner assembles one character from bits received over the communication line before interrupting the CCU.

o   Type 3 Scanner: This scanner can hold up to 8 characters in its internal buffers from bits received over a communication line before interrupting the CCU.

In what follows, we shall describe the operation of the Type 2 scanners. There are several points of similarity in the operation of all three types of scanners and an understanding of the operation of Type 2 will provide the reader with an overview of the principles of scanner operation.

A 3705 can support up to four Type 2 Scanners. The scanners are attached to the CCU via a Type 2 Attachment Base. A communication line is attached to the scanner via a line set (also called an interface) and a line interface base (LIB), as shown in Figure 11-12.

Each scanner can support up to 6 line interface bases and each LIB can support up to 16 line sets; a Type 2 Scanner can support up to 96 half-duplex lines. The functions of the LIB are to provide bit clocking and to drive and terminate all signals between communication scanners and line sets. A line set provides the hardware connection between LIB and the communication line. A single line set can provide the interface for one full-duplex or two half-duplex communication lines. Start/Stop, BSC and SDLC protocols are supported.

There is a 48 bit Interface Control Word (ICW) in the scanner for every line attached to the LIB (there are 96 ICWs, corresponding to 96 lines). The ICW corresponding to a line contains several fields that are important to the operation of a scanner. Figure 11-13 shows the format and fields used by the ICW. The Secondary Control Field is used for holding sensing and control data. The Parallel Data Field serves as a buffer for holding one character. The Line Control Definer Field contains flags for BSC, SDLC, and Start/Stop interfaces. The Primary Control Field represents the state of interface at any given time. The Serial Data Field is used to assemble bits as they are received from a line or to disassemble bits if they are to be transmitted by a line. For receive operations, when a character has been assembled in the Serial Data Field, it is transferred under hardware control to the Parallel Data Field. For transmit operations, a character from the Parallel Data Field is first transferred under hardware control to the Serial Data Field and subsequently each bit is moved to the line interface under hardware control.

In addition to ICWs, there are two more registers called the ICW Work Register and the ICW Input Register that are used for intermediate storage in various operations.

Each line attached to a scanner has a unique 9 bit address, with the first two bits specifying the scanner

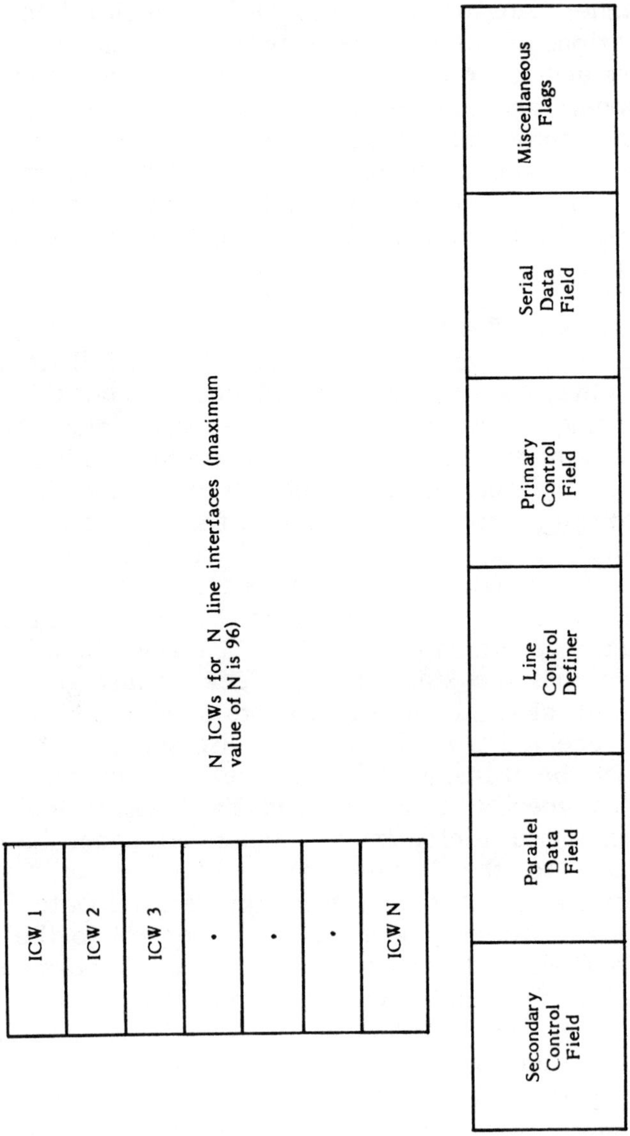

Figure 11-13/Format of the ICW

address and the next three bits speci-fying the line address (see Figure 11-14). The 3705 can address a total of 352 lines in the maximal configuration, and 9 bits are needed to address this many lines.

The attachment base to which the scanner is connected has a continuously running scan counter that generates a line address which is sent simultaneously to all the scanners connected to that attachment base (see Figure 11-15). Each scanner uses the line address to load the corresponding ICW into the ICW Work Register; the scanner hardware checks to see if a character has been assembled in the ICW and, in such a case, the scanner hardware decides that interrupt action is necessary. It initiates a request for a level 2 interrupt and the CCU gets the line address from the attachment base (specifically, from a register called Attachment Buffer Address Register (ABAR)) and the contents of the ICW from the ICW Input Register. If the scanner hardware decides that no interrupt action is to be taken, the ICW is replaced and the scanner waits for the next address.

The time required by the scanner to scan the interface address is 1.6 microseconds; 96 lines can be scanned during a total time of 153.6 microseconds. This imposes restrictions on line speeds: a Type 2 Scanner cannot handle line speeds of more than 4800 bits per second without having bit overruns. The addressing can be speeded up in certain cases by a technique called address substitution under which certain lines can be addressed more often than others.

We shall next discuss briefly the method of operation of a Type 3 Scanner, which is similar to that of a Type 2 Scanner except that the following modifications improve scanner performance:

1)   The scanner has additional local storage that can hold eight characters of data for each line.

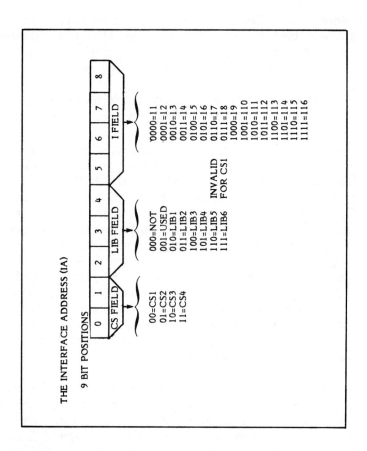

LEGEND:

CS - Communication Scanner

LIB - Line Interface Board

I - Interface to Communication Line

Figure 11-14/Line Interface Addressing

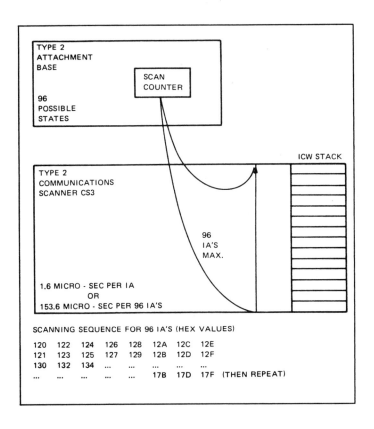

SCANNING SEQUENCE FOR 96 IA'S (HEX VALUES)

120	122	124	126	128	12A	12C	12E	
121	123	125	127	129	12B	12D	12F	
130	132	134	...	...	...	...	...	
...	...	...	...	...	17B	17D	17F	(THEN REPEAT)

Figure 11-15/Scanning Sequence

2)   The scanner transfers data to main storage without CCU intervention by means of cycle stealing.

3)   The scanner can support high speed lines by generating their addresses more frequently for scanning purposes.

In regard to modification (1) the parallel data field (PDF) of the ICW can hold eight bytes of data, as compared to one byte of data in the case of the Type 2 Scanner.

Modification (2) frees the CCU to perform other functions while data transfer takes place. The scanner steals storage cycles from CCU when it performs data transfer to and from main storage. Two bytes are transferred at one time between main storage and the PDF. The CCU cannot perform storage operations while the cycle steal operation is in progress but it can execute instructions involving registers. Thus, the CCU does not have to be entirely tied-up when a data transfer is in progress, as in the case of the Type 2 Scanner. The scanner hardware removes data from the PDF into the serial data field (SDF) and this data is moved into the line interface hardware for bit-by-bit transmission, as in the case of the Type 2 Scanner.

As regards modification (3), the Type 3 Scanner uses the same attachment base as a Type 2 Scanner. Under normal scanner operation, a Type 3 Scanner examines 96 interface addresses but the scanner operation can be modified in two ways, namely (1) by placing an upper limit on the address generated and (2) by substituting addresses assigned to the first line interface base to be substituted in place of a sequentially generated address. The idea underlying address modification and placing a ceiling on generated addresses is to support high speed lines.

Channel Adapters.   A channel adapter provides the means for connecting the 3705 to the host channel. It has the necessary hardware circuits for monitoring the channel for one or several addresses that are assigned to it and also for performing data transfer between the channel and the 3705. From the channel's point of view, the channel adapter behaves like a control unit and the sequence of initial selection, data transfer and final status presentation described in Chapter 10 is observed. There are four types of channel adapters (Type 1 to Type 4) and their functional characteristics are described in Figure 11-16.

As mentioned previously, there are two modes of operation of the 3705 known as emulation mode (ESC) and native mode (NSC). If the emulation mode (ESC) is used the 3705 emulates a 270X Transmission Control Unit (TCU). Under this mode, the channel adapter is required to work with a range of subchannel addresses since every line is assigned a unique subchannel address. Under the native mode (NSC) the channel adapter works with only one subchannel address.

A 3705 can have up to 4 channel adapters of various types. Types 1 and 4 can be used in both ESC and NSC modes and transfer data in bursts; a program interrupt occurs in the Central Control Unit after the transfer of each burst of data. Types 2 and 3 can be used only in the NSC mode and an interruption takes place after completion of the entire data transfer.

In what follows, we shall describe the Type 4 channel adapter under the ESC mode and the Type 3 channel adapter under the NSC mode. The operation of the Type 1 channel adapter is quite similar to that of the Type 4; the Type 2 channel adapter is similar to the Type 3. Also, the ESC and NSC modes of operation are identical in most respects.

The operation of the Type 4 channel adapter in the emulation mode can be broken down into the following phases:

1. Types -- There are 4 types of channel adapters, Types 1, 2, 3, 4; any one of them can be used under native mode.

2. Channels -- The following channels can be used:

   Byte Multiplexer -- Types 1, 2, 3, 4

   Block Multiplexer -- Types 2, 3, 4

   Selector -- Types 2 and 4

3. Data Transfer -- Data is read from or written to the 3705 main storage in two modes:

   o   Cycle Steal -- Types 2, 3, 4

   o   Bursts of Data -- Types 1, 4

4. Two Channel Switch -- Types 1, 2, and 4 have a 2 channel switch (a manual switch) which permits 2 channels to be connected to a channel adapter; however, only one channel can be enabled for operations at one time. Type 3 has a 2 channel interface for attachment to two processors (i.e., the channel adapter can be shared by 2 processors).

Figure 11-16/Characteristics of Channel Adapters

Monitoring Phase. The channel adapter continually monitors the channel for a set of assigned subchannel addresses. When it encounters one of these addresses, it enters the initial selection phase.

Initial Selection Phase. During this phase, the channel adapter stores the channel command and the device address in a register called Initial Selection Address and Command Register (ISACR). The command word is checked for parity error and an initial status byte is presented to the channel. A level 3 interrupt of the CPU is requested by the channel adapter.

Data Transfer Phase. When data is transferred from the 3705 to the host, the following steps take place:

a)   The I/O device (i.e., the terminal) address is loaded to a channel adapter register.

b)   The first 2 bytes of data are placed in a data buffer register of the channel adapter.

c)   The next 2 bytes of data are placed in a data buffer register of the channel adapter.

d)   A register in the channel adapter called Data/Status Control Register (DSCR) is set in various bit patterns to indicate the direction of the data transfer (from channel adapter to host), the byte count, and other related items.

e)   The channel adapter goes into a hardware-controlled sequence during which it alerts the channel that it requires service and transfers data. At the end of the data transfer, it notifies the CCU with a level 3 interrupt.

When data is transferred from the host to the 3705, the following steps take place:

a)   The I/O device address is presented to the channel adapter.

b)   The channel adapter transfers up to 4 bytes of data from the channel using hardware-controlled logic.

c)   At the end of the data transfer, the channel adapter causes an interrupt to the CCU.

Final Status Transfer Phase.   As mentioned before, the initial selection status is hardware generated by the channel adapter.   The final status is generated by the control program in the CCU. For normal operations, channel and device end bits are set by the control program.

In the ESC mode, the device address is also presented along with the status.

The Type 3 channel adapter supports only the NSC mode. Its main characteristics are the following:

1)   It uses only one subchannel address.

2)   It uses a cycle steal mode of operation in data transfer to the 3705 main storage.

As mentioned in the section on Type 3 scanners, a cycle steal operation allows a device to transfer data directly to main storage without the registers of the processor being used in the process.   The device "steals" cycles from the processor, meaning that the processor cannot access storage while the data transfer is in progress. The processor, however, can execute instructions that do not involve storage access.

During a cycle steal operation, two bytes of data are transferred directly to the 3705 main storage from the channel adapter at the end of a CCU cycle. In the absence of cycle steal, the channel adapter has to interrupt the CPU for performing data transfer operations between channel adapter and main storage.

A functional description of the Type 3 channel adapter is given in Figure 11-17.

11.3 IBM 3270 INFORMATION DISPLAY SYSTEM

The IBM 3270 Information Display System is a family of terminals, printers, and control units that offer a wide range of capabilities and a variety of configurations. The three components within the system are the following:

o   Control Unit

o   Display Station

o   Printer

The display station can have screen buffers of 480 or 1920 characters. The primary unit of display is a field, which is preceded by an attribute character as shown in Figure 11-18. The attribute specifies whether the field is protected or unprotected, alphanumeric or numeric, and so forth. Null characters (all zero bits) separate fields and are stored in the buffer but are not used in data transmission. The keyboard, in addition to the usual typewriter keys, has a set of Program Function (PF) keys numbered from one to twelve, which can be used for special functions assigned to it by the on-line application program controlling the data entry. PF keys are generally used for scrolling, clearing panels and for invoking menus.

A control unit may be housed with the display station in the case of certain models (e.g., IBM 3275). In other models, the control unit is housed separately and is attached to display stations and printers. The 3271 control unit, for example, can be attached to a maximum of 32 display stations and printers.

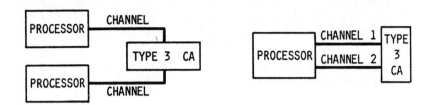

1. Characteristics:

   o   Cycle steal data transfer

   o   Dual channel interfacing capability

2. Method of operation:

   o   <u>Transfer From Host</u>
        -    Channel issues following commands:
             a)   TEST I/O (to see if CA is free or busy
                   - CA responds with busy or free
                   status)
             c)   WRITE (data transfer from the host
                   takes place)

   o   <u>Transfer to Host</u>
        -    Channel adapter issues an attention inter-
             ruption
        -    Host issues a Start I/O for reading

Figure 11-17/Functional Description of Type 3 Channel
Adapter

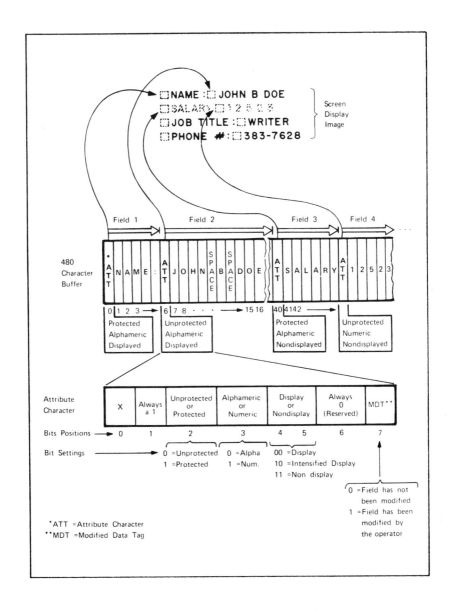

Figure 11-18/Display Station Buffer

In a local attachment, the control unit is connected to the channel as shown in Figure 11-19. The processes of selection, initial status byte presentation and data transfer follow the rules described in Chapter 10. In a remote attachment, control units are multidropped from a communication line originating from the 3705 as shown in Figure 11-20. The 3705 is the control station and the 3270 control units are tributaries. Each control unit is polled or selected in the manner described below:

Polling. Each control unit monitors the line for its polling address and a general poll or a specific poll can be sent down the line.

A general poll is an invitation to the control unit to send data from any display station attached to it. In such a case, the control unit interrogates in turn each station to see if it has any data to send and acknowledges the poll if a station has data to send.

A specific poll is an invitation to send data from a specific display station. The control unit interrogates the station and responds positively to the poll if the station has data to send.

Selection. Each control unit monitors its selection address which specifies also the address of a display station. In other words, selection is always specific, unlike polling which can be either general or specific.

Local Operation. In the case of local attachment, the host issues a start I/O operation for initiating I/O activity. This results in the execution of a channel program. The commands that are used in this context are grouped into the categories, namely READ and WRITE commands.

A READ command is used for transferring data from the 3270 to main storage and a WRITE command is used for transferring data from main storage to the 3270.

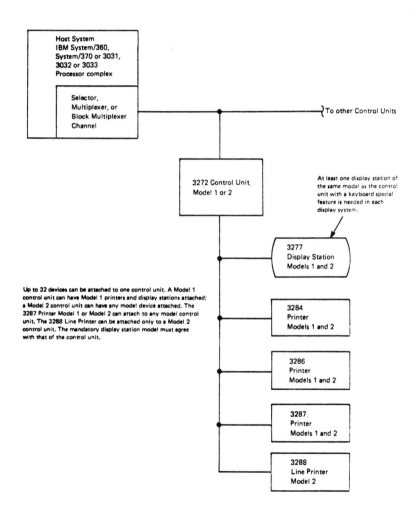

Figure 11-19/Local Attachment of a 3270

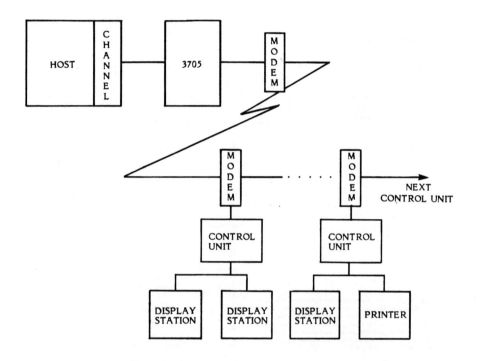

Figure 11-20/Remote 3270 Configuration

The data that is transferred consists of screen data, orders and special characters. The screen data is data that is entered or read by the terminal operator. Orders are used for the control of the display station buffer and the printer. Special characters are used for carrying additional information, as explained later.

The most commonly used READ command is the READ MODIFIED command which reads only those fields in the screen that are modified by the operator, thereby eliminating unnecessary transfer of data that has not been changed in any way. Figure 11-22 shows the input data stream for the screen shown earlier in Figure 11-18. This data is transmitted by the 3270 control unit via the channel to main storage. The first character that is present in the input data stream is an attention ID (AID) character. The AID is a special character and its function is to provide interruption handling routine with information regarding the type of routine that should process the data from the terminal. An operator can, after modifying data on the screen, press ENTER, CLEAR or a few other keys for indicating that the screen is to be transmitted (see Figure 11-23). The AID byte contains a code for the spcific key that is pressed and is used by the host communication software to execute the appropriate program for processing the data received from the terminal.

The next two bytes in the input data stream are also special characters and contain information about the position of the cursor which is necessary for subsequent screen control.

The rest of the data consists of screen data and orders. A frequently used buffer control order is Set Buffer Address (SBA). The purpose of this order is to show the position of the field in the buffer — which is necessary since only modified parts in the buffer are transmitted.

The output data stream used in conjunction with the WRITE command begins with a special character called Write Control Character (WCC) which contains bit confi-

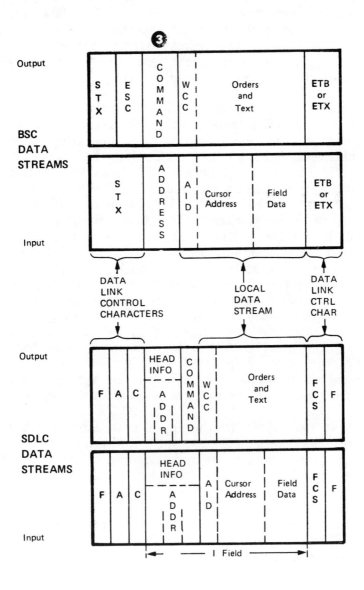

Figure 11-21/Data Streams Between Communications
Controller and 3270 Control Unit

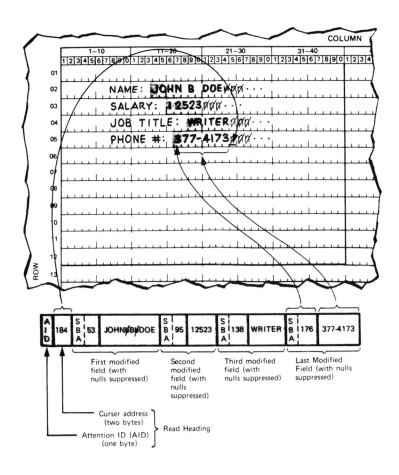

Figure 11-22/Input Data Stream for a Read Modified
Operation

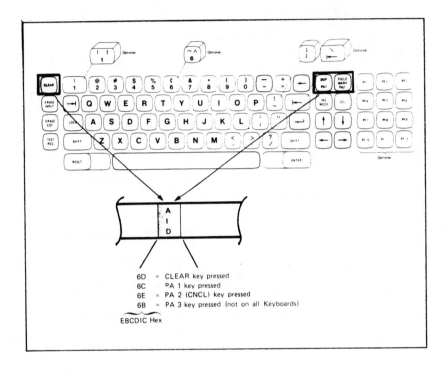

Figure 11-23/Explanation of AID

gurations for starting the printer, sounding the audible alarm and other such functions. The rest of the data consists of screen data and orders. In addition to SBA, the output data stream frequently uses orders for repositioning the cursor (Insert Cursor), for specifying that the next character is an attribute character (e.g., a character indicating that the field should be displayed using high intensity) and similar buffer control functions.

Remote Method of Operation. In the case of remote attachment, the host or the communications controller (3705) performs the polling and selection operations, depending on whether the emulation or native mode is used.

Figure 11-21 shows the input and output data streams used in connection with BSC and SDLC. If BSC is used, in the case of a read operation the input data stream sent by the control unit to the 3705 or the host is shown in Figure 11-21. The control unit adds the BSC control characters STX and ETX and an address (indicating control unit and device) to the local output data stream which we have explained already. Similarly, in the case of SDLC, data link control characters and address are added to the local data stream.

Let us take the case of the write operation next. Figure 11-21 shows the output data stream sent by the 3705 to the 3270 control unit. The data stream consists of data link control characters (e.g., STX, ESC, ETX), a write command and local output data stream comprising the WCC byte plus orders and text. The ESC character sets the control unit from the monitoring mode into a text receiving mode and the control unit reads the rest of the output data stream. The control unit strips all data link characters before passing the output data stream to the display station which is specified in the address given in the selection sequence.

We shall not go into any more details regarding 3270 operation. The interested reader is referred to the bibliography at the end of Part III.

12 IBM Disk Storage Control Units and Disk Drives

Our next topic of discussion is the control units and devices pertaining to disk systems.

A disk system consists of the following components:

o   control units usually called storage controls

o   a set of disk drives attached to the control units

Figure 12-1 shows a commonly used physical configuration of a disk system. The host is connected to a storage control via a block multiplexer (or selector) channel. The storage control is connected to two strings of disk drives. A string is a set of disk drives the first of which (called the head of string) has certain control and power capabilities. We shall be discussing examples of strings in the section on the IBM 3350.

Figure 12-2 shows a shared direct access storage device (DASD) configuration in which a string is attached to more than one control unit and control units are attached to more than one channel; there are two CPUs in the configuration, with a channel belonging to each CPU. Under this configuration, a device (i.e., a disk drive) can be accessed by more than one I/O path.

12.1 ORGANIZATION OF DISK DRIVES

Before we discuss specific control units and devices we shall describe the basic characteristics of disk systems. A disk drive consists of a stack of recording disks, and each recording disk has two surfaces (called data surfaces) available for recording data. Each data surface is logically organized into concentric circles called tracks for recording data. A track is broken into arcs called records. The set of tracks of a specified radius resident on

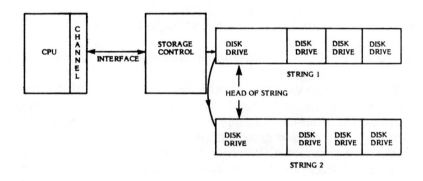

Figure 12-1/Non-shared Configuration for Disk Drives

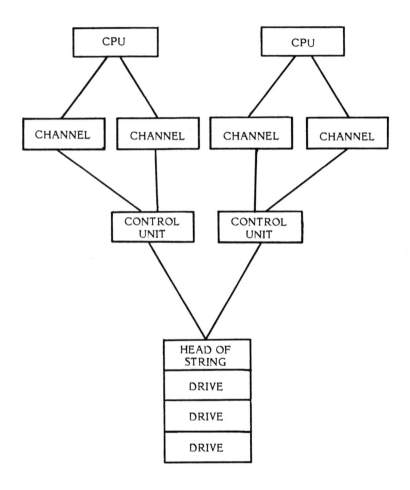

Figure 12-2/Shared DASD

all data surfaces is called a cylinder. The hierarchy of data organization in a disk drive has the following levels:

o   disk drive

o   cylinder

o   track

o   record

In other words, the data in a disk drive is composed of cylinders which consist of tracks and the tracks, in turn, are composed of records. Figures 12-3 through 12-5 illustrate the organization of data on a disk drive.

One or more read/write head is used to store and retrieve data from a data surface. The disk drive rotates about its axis with a constant speed and the read/write head can be either fixed or moving, as explained next.

Fixed Head Configuration. In a fixed head configuration, there is a read/write head corresponding to every track; the read/write heads are positioned immediately above the tracks and remain stationary while the disk drive rotates about its axis. The primary delay associated with accessing a record in a track is caused by the rotational time taken by the disk drive so that the record comes under the read/write head (this time is called rotational delay).

Moving Head Configuration. In a moving head configuration, there is no longer a one-to-one correspondence between a track and a read/write head. A read/write head is assigned to several tracks on a disk surface (e.g., in the case of the IBM 3350 two read/write heads are assigned per disk surface) and has to move radially across the disk surface to reach a track. The delay associated with accessing a record on a track consists of the following major components:

1)   The time required to position the read/write head

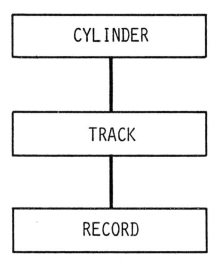

Figure 12-3/Data Organization (Logical) on a Disk Drive

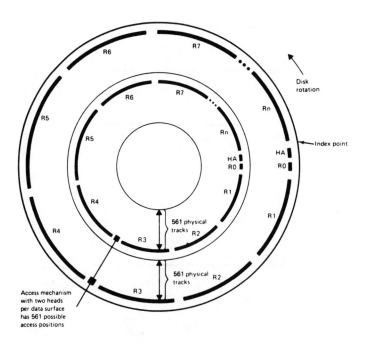

Figure 12-4/Tracks and Records on a Recording Surface

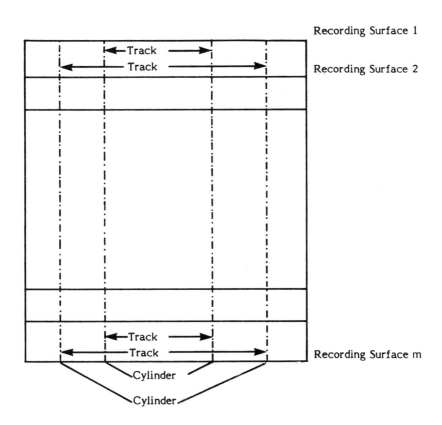

Figure 12-5/Cylinder/Track Relationship

over the specified track, called seek time;

2) The time required for the disk drive to rotate so that the specified record comes under the read/ write head, called rotational delay (same as for a fixed head configuration).

Track Layout. The general layout of a track is illustrated in Figure 12-6; for the detailed track layout of an IBM 3350, see Figure 12-17. An index marker indicates the beginning of a track. A track is composed of records which are separated by gaps. A record consists of the following elements:

o   count area

o   key area

o   data area

A record may be of variable length and hence its length is stored in the count area; it may have a key in which case the key area contains the same. The data area, as its name implies, contains the actual data present in the record plus error correction code bytes.

The inter-record and intra-record gaps are used for providing time intervals for channels and control units to perform their functions. For instance, command chaining requires that the channel fetch the next CCW from main storage, decode it and pass it on to the control unit. The channel and control unit perform these operations during the time it takes for a gap to move under the read/write head.

The home address contains the physical address of the track and its condition. It is followed by record, R0, which is called the track descriptor record. Its main function is to define the address of an alternate track if the track is defective, and to provide the address of the defective track in the case of an alternate track.

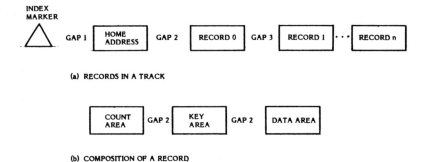

Figure 12-6/Track and Record Layout

Addressing. A record can be uniquely specified by a cylinder number, a track number (also called head) within the cylinder and a record number (called record ID) within the track. The record ID is contained in the count area of the record. A record address consists of five bytes and is represented by means of the notation of CC HH R where CC represents the 2 byte cylinder address, HH represents the two byte track address, and R represents the one byte record ID. A record can be located by using the CC HH R address or by specifying a key value which is located in the key area of the record. See the section on Channel, Control Unit and Device Interaction for descriptions of search operations.

Sectors and Rotational Position Sensing. A disk surface is divided into equal sectors, as shown in Figure 12-7. Rotational position sensing (RPS) is the ability of the device to sense the arrival of a specified sector under the read/write head. We have seen in earlier sections that the block multiplexer channel can perform control operations on several devices concurrently. With RPS, a drive can disconnect itself from the block multiplexer channel during the rotational delay required before the specified sector appears under the read/write head.

Suppose it is desired to read a record with a given cylinder, track, and record ID and assume that RPS is not available. The cylinder and track are chosen and every record in that track is examined to see if the IDs match. This means that the channel has to be attached to the device for the entire search operation. With RPS, a sector corresponding to the record is specified by a SET SECTOR command in the channel program and the disk drive can disconnect during the time it takes for the sector to appear under the read/write head (when an alert is issued to the channel). If the channel is not ready, the device goes through one more rotation and alerts the channel again before the sector appears under the read/write head.

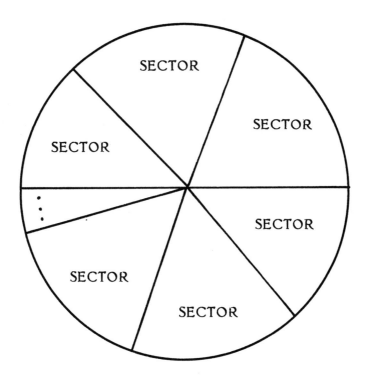

Figure 12-7/Sectors on a Disk Surface

It should be pointed out that sectors are not physically marked out on data surfaces but are identified in the time that is required for a sector to be traversed by the read/write head as the disk rotates at constant speed. For example, the sector time for a 3350 is approximately 130 microseconds since the time for a full revolution is 16.7 milliseconds and there are 128 sectors on a data surface.

12.2 FUNCTIONS OF A STORAGE CONTROL

The function of a storage control (i.e., a disk control unit) varies according to implementation, and in this chapter we are restricting ourselves to the more recent IBM storage control units (e.g., IBM 3830) which have microprograms of their own to perform sophisticated disk management functions. The microprograms use registers and control storage which are housed in the storage control itself. In general, the following functions are performed by a storage control:

o   device selection

o   CCW execution

o   status presentation
o   error detection and correction

o   command retry

o   multiple requesting

o   multi-track operation

o   rotational position sensing

o   channel switching

o   string switching (actually, a feature of the string)

We shall describe these functions in the following paragraphs.

Device Selection. When the CPU issues a Start I/O instruction, the channel fetches the first CCW from main storage. Next, the channel sends the control unit and device address specified by the Start I/O instruction to all storage controls attached to it. The storage control, having matching address checks to see if the addressed device (i.e., a disk drive), is available for use. The control unit notifies the channel of the status of the device, whether it is available for use, busy, or not operational. If the device is available for use, the channel passes the CCW to the control unit which presents the channel with an initial status byte (see the section on Channel, Control Unit and Device Interaction for a more detailed account of an I/O operation).

Status Presentation. The storage control presents the channel with status bytes at various stages of an I/O operation. An initial status byte (normally all bits zero) is presented after device selection and receipt of the first CCW, as mentioned under Device Selection. An ending status byte is presented after the execution of every CCW and this contains the channel end and device end flags for most operations.

CCW Execution. The storage control executes one channel command at a time. The following categories of channel commands are applicable for disk operations:

- search

- read

- write

- sense

- control

These commands are discussed in the section on channel, control unit and disk interaction.

The storage control interprets a command and gives instructions to the device.

Error Detection and Correction. An odd parity bit is used by the channel in transferring a byte to the control unit (i.e., the bit is set to 1 if there is an even number of one bits within a byte), and the control unit checks the parity bit for error detection.

The control unit removes the parity bit and adds error correction code (ECC) bytes which are computed and written for each recorded area in a track. During a read operation, the ECC bytes are recalculated and compared with the existing ECC bytes to detect errors. In case of errors, the CCW is re-executed using the Command Retry facility.

Command Retry. This feature pertains to the channel and/or control unit and enables the re-execution of a CCW in a channel program in the case of an error. The retry is automatic and does not cause a CPU interruption or the use of programmed error recovery routines.

Multiple Track Operation. This facility enables the control unit to automatically select the next track (in ascending sequence of numbers) when the track that is presently under the read/write head has come to an end. If a record cannot be found in a given track as a result of a search operation, the next track is automatically scanned. Thus, the necessity for using another seek command in the channel program in order to position the read/write head on a new track (within the cylinder) is eliminated.

Record Overflow. A record may be larger than a track and may span more than one track. The portion of a record contained in a track is called a record segment. Each track contains, in such a situation, an R0 record and the count and key of the record segment in that track, as shown in Figure 12-6. The tracks have to be specially formatted using a write special count, key, and data command (CKD). A flag byte in the count area indicates that a record is an overflow segment. Figure 12-8 describes typical channel programs for reading and writing overflow records.

Note that the size of a record cannot exceed a cylinder and a record cannot span two or more cylinders.

Multiple Requesting. The multiple requesting capability enables a block multiplexer channel to perform concurrent I/O operations on drives belonging to the same string. Assume that the channel is executing a channel program initiated by a Start I/O operation and that a seek or a set sector command is being executed. During the rotational delay necessary before the record appears under the read/write head, the drive disconnects itself and if the multiple requesting capability is present in the control unit a Start I/O operation on another drive can be initiated before the completion of the previous operation.

Channel Switching. If a storage control has the channel switching feature, it can be connected to more than one channel. Storage Controls having two or four channel switches are available currently.

We shall describe the operation of a storage control having a two-channel switch; the logic is the same for storage controls having more than two channel switches.

The storage control has two toggle switches which can be set manually. When both switches are on, both channels can access drives via the storage control; when a switch is off, only one channel can access drives via the storage control. Assuming that both switches are on, only one channel can use the storage control at any given time. During the time that the channel stays connected to a storage control, no other channel can select the storage control and a busy status is returned if such selection is made. In the

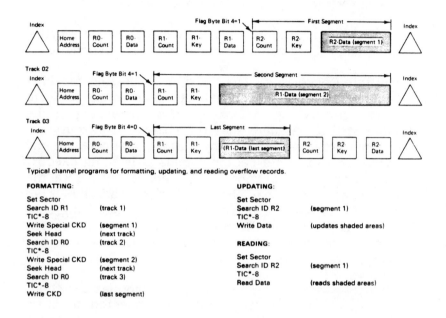

Typical channel programs for formatting, updating, and reading overflow records.

FORMATTING:

Set Sector	
Search ID R1	(track 1)
TIC*-8	
Write Special CKD	(segment 1)
Seek Head	(next track)
Search ID R0	(track 2)
TIC*-8	
Write Special CKD	(segment 2)
Seek Head	(next track)
Search ID R0	(track 3)
TIC*-8	
Write CKD	(last segment)

UPDATING:

Set Sector	
Search ID R2	(segment 1)
TIC*-8	
Write Data	(updates shaded areas)

READING:

Set Sector	
Search ID R2	(segment 1)
TIC*-8	
Read Data	(reads shaded areas)

Figure 12-8/Record Overflow Illustration

case of a block multiplexer channel, the drive disconnects from the channel during motion of the read/write head or rotational delay.

To prevent two channels from updating data on a disk drive concurrently, a channel program can reserve a device by means of a Device Reserve command (one of the SENSE commands). A reserved device can be subsequently released by means of a Device Release command. A device that is reserved by a channel cannot be used by any other channel until it is released.

See Figure 12-9 for a concise description of channel switching.

String Switching. String switching is a feature of the disk string and not of the storage control. However, we shall discuss it here on account of the similarity between string switching and channel switching.

A string of disk drives can be connected to more than one storage control if it has the string switching capability. Assume that two storage controls are connected to a string; any one storage control can select and reserve a specific drive using the Device Reserve command and subsequently release it by means of a Device Release command.

A concise description of string switching is given in Figure 12-10. A description of shared DASD arising from channel switching or string switching is given in Figure 12-11.

12.3 CHANNEL, STORAGE CONTROL AND DISK DRIVE INTERRACTION

Let us assume that the CPU has issued a Start I/O instruction in order to perform a read or write operation from a disk drive.

1. Definition -- When a control unit (with a 2-or-4-channel switch) is connected to more than one channel, the resulting I/O operations are done by channel switching.

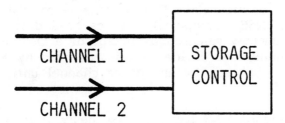

2. Operation -- A channel reserves a device for its own use by using a device reserve CCW; the device is freed by means of the device release CCW.

3. Use -- Channel switching is mostly used for providing alternate I/O path to a device.

Figure 12-9/Channel Switching

1. String -- A string is a set of disk drives, with a controller called head of string. For example, in the case of the IBM 3350, a string appears as follows:

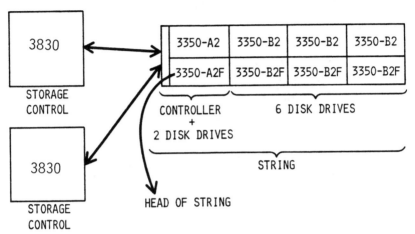

2. String Switch -- The storage control functions as a control unit and can be connected to up to 4 strings. The controller in each string has a programmable switch which enables it to switch to either one of two storage control units.

Figure 12-10/String Switching

1. Definition -- A drive in a string that is accessible to
    two or more processors because of multiple I/O paths
    created by channel-switching or string-switching
    capabilities is called shared DASD.

2. Operation -- A storage control unit can select and
    reserve a drive using a device reserve CCW; and when
    no longer needed, the device can be freed using a
    device release CCW. Likewise, a channel can reserve
    a control unit by using a device reserve CCW and
    release it by a device release CCW.

3. Use -- Shared DASD is mostly used when common
    system data (catalogs, program libraries) have to be
    shared by multiple processors.

Figure 12-11/Shared DASD

COMMAND	COMMAND CODE			
	Multitrack Off		Multitrack On	
	Hex	Binary	Hex	Binary
CONTROL				
No Operation	03	0000 0011		
Recalibrate	13	0001 0011		
Seek	07	0000 0111		
Seek Cylinder	0B	0000 1011		
Seek Head	1B	0001 1011		
Space Count	0F	0000 1111		
Set File Mask	1F	0001 1111		
Set Sector	23	0010 0011		
Restore	17	0001 0111		
Transfer In Channel	x8*	xxxx 1000		
Diagnostic Load	53	0101 0011		
Diagnostic Write	73	0111 0011		
SEARCH				
Home Address Equal	39	0011 1001	B9	1011 1001
Identifier ID Equal	31	0011 0001	B1	1011 0001
Identifier ID High	51	0101 0001	D1	1101 0001
Identifier ID Equal or High	71	0111 0001	F1	1111 0001
Key Equal	29	0010 1001	A9	1010 1001
Key High	49	0100 1001	C9	1100 1001
Key Equal or High	69	0110 1001	E9	1110 1001
READ				
Home Address	1A	0001 1010	9A	1001 1010
Count	12	0001 0010	92	1001 0010
Record Zero (R0)	16	0001 0110	96	1001 0110
Data	06	0000 0110	86	1000 0110
Key and Data	0E	0000 1110	8E	1000 1110
Count, Key, and Data	1E	0001 1110	9E	1001 1110
Multiple Count, Key, and Data**	5E	0101 1110	.	.
IPL	02	0000 0010		
Sector	22	0010 0010	.	.
SENSE				
Input/Output (I/O) Type**	E4	1110 0100		
Input/Output (I/O)	04	0000 0100		
Read and Reset Buffered Log	A4	1010 0100		
Device Reserve	B4	1011 0100		
Unconditional Reserve***	14	0001 0100		
Device Release	94	1001 0100		
Read Diagnostic Status 1	44	0100 0100		
WRITE				
Home Address	19	0001 1001		
Record Zero (R0)	15	0001 0101		
Erase	11	0001 0001		
Count, Key, and Data	1D	0001 1101		
Special Count, Key, and Data	01	0000 0001		
Data	05	0000 0101		
Key and Data	0D	0000 1101		

*   x not significant (addresses should not exceed storage capacity).
**   Available only if 3830-2 uses microcode supporting 3344 or 3350 devices.
***   Available only if 3830-2 uses microcode supporting 3350 devices.

Use of command codes other than shown causes unit check in initial status. A subsequent sense operation indicates command reject.

Figure 12-12/Table of Command Codes

The channel reads the first channel command word (CCW) from main storage and selects the device (whose address is specified in the I/O instruction) by sending the address to all control units attached to the channel. Note that the address specified in the I/O instruction (one byte in length) contains both control unit and device addresses. The control unit, on receiving its address, responds to the channel and the channel sends it the command code of the CCW. The control unit presents an initial status byte to the channel which the channel presents to the CPU; the Start I/O intstruction is completed at this stage, freeing the CPU to perform other functions.

If command chaining is specified in the first CCW, the channel fetches the next CCW from main storage and passes it to the control unit which, in turn, sends it to the device. Most disk operations use several chained CCWs comprising a channel program.

Typical Commands. The channel commands pertaining to disk I/O operation can be divided into the following categories:

- SEARCH commands

- READ commands

- WRITE commands

- SENSE/TEST commands

- CONTROL commands

A table showing commands and their codes used with 3350 disk drives is given in Figure 12-12.

The function of a SEARCH command is to locate a record satisfying a given search criterion. The following are examples of search criteria:

o   SEARCH ID EQUAL -- A record identifier in the form (CC HH R) is given at the data address specified in the CCW and the control unit compares this ID with the count area ID of the record recently read by the device.

o   SEARCH ID HIGH -- The same as above, except that record ID should be higher than ID specified by the CCW.

o   SEARCH KEY EQUAL -- A key identifier is given at the data address specified by the CCW and the control unit compares this value with the key area of the record recently read by the device.

If the search criterion is satisfied, the control unit presents channel end, device end and status modifier bits to the channel; if the search criterion is not satisfied, the control unit presents only channel end and device end bits to the channel. The status modifier flag (indicating that the search has been satisfied) causes the channel to skip the next CCW and execute the succeeding CCW. In other words, branching in channel programs is caused by the presentation of the status modifier flag. The following CCW sequence is commonly used in disk channel programs:

1.   Search ID Equal

2.   TIC* - 8

3.   Read Data

The first CCW specifies a search for a record with a given ID in the CC HH R format. The control unit compares the ID of the last record read with the specified value and presents a channel end, device end, and status modifier to the channel on an equal comparison. Because the status modifier is presented, the channel skips the second CCW and fetches the third CCW for reading data. (Notice that the gap between the count area containing the ID and the data area containing the data allows a time interval during which the control unit presents the channel with channel end, device end and status modifier bits and which permits the channel to execute the read CCW.) On unequal comparison, the status modifier is not presented and the channel executes the second CCW which is a transfer-in-channel command that enables the first CCW to be executed again. TIC*-8 is shorthand notation for indicating that the next CCW to be executed is 8 bytes lower than the address of the transfer-in-channel CCW; in other words, TIC*-8 indicates that the last CCW is to be re-executed.

To summarize, the SEARCH command in conjunction with the transfer-in-channel command enables looping and branching in a channel program with the intention of continuing the search until the search criterion is satisfied (see also section 5.6 on channel programs).

The READ command is used to transfer data from the device to the main storage. The data is transferred serially bit by bit from the device to the control unit and one byte at a time from the control unit to the channel.

The control unit usually checks for the validity of data by examining error correction code (ECC) bytes.

At the end of data transfer, the control unit presents an ending status byte containing channel end and device end.

The WRITE commands are of two kinds, namely (1) for formatting tracks and records and (2) for updating an existing record.

The formatting write commands are used for initializing tracks and records and also for specifying the sizes of the various areas in a record like key area, data area, etc. During initialization, error correction code bytes are written after each area.

The write update commands are used for data transfer

from main storage to the device and the tracks have to be formatted before using these commands.

The SENSE/TEST commands are used for ascertaining the status of a device and usually results in the control unit presenting a status byte to the channel.

The CONTROL commands are used for various seek operations and for setting sectors and file masks. A seek can be for a specified cylinder or a cylinder and head. The seek command can be followed by a read command to examine all the records in a track and to select a record that meets certain criteria. The same result is achieved quicker by using a search command, but in certain cases it may be preferable to seek and read records sequentially.

The SET SECTOR command is used if the rotational position sensing feature is to be used advantageously. It may be possible to specify a sector number that appears under the read/write head slightly before the record itself makes its appearance; in such a case, the drive can disconnect itself from the channel during the rotational delay prior to the appearance of the sector. The channel is alerted before the sector is due for appearance and can reconnect to perform operations like searching, reading, etc. In the event that a sector number corresponding to a record cannot be established easily, a sector address of zero can be specified which corresponds to the beginning of the track (positioned by the index).

Another control command of interest is the SET FILE MASK whose function is to specify subsequent permissible disk operations by means of a mask byte. The bits in the mask byte can specify admissible and non-admissible operations, examples of which are given below:

o   write commands

o   seek commands

o   write R0

The set file mask is used as a means of protection for accidental destruction of data on the disk.

We shall now proceed to give an example of a channel program for reading a record from a disk. Let us consider the following sequence:

Seek

Set Sector

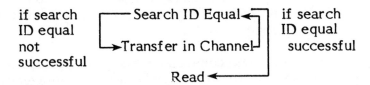

The above is a sequence of IBM 3350 commands whose functions are:

1)   Seek -- The access mechanism is moved to the cylinder specified by the seek address and the head specified by the seek address is selected.

2)   Set Sector -- A sector number (0-127) indicating the angular track position is specified, to be used in conjunction with the rotational position sensing mechanism.

3)   Search ID Equal -- This command attempts to locate a count area in a track having the matching CCHHR address.

4)   Read -- Transfers data area or record from disk to main storage.

Figure 12-13 indicates the CPU, channel, control unit and device interaction in the case of a block multiplexer channel. The CPU issues an SIO instruction and is free for other activity after device selection. Note that if SIOF had been used, the CPU would have been freed up earlier since SIOF assumes that the device is free and available for use and hence its completion does not depend on device selection; if it turns out later that the device is not free, an I/O interruption is presented by the channel.

The first CCW of the channel program shown in Figure 12-13 is a SEEK. The seek address is transferred from the channel to the control unit and the control unit presents a channel end (CE) after the seek address transfer. The channel is free to service other control units and devices. The control unit initiates a seek operation on the disk and after the head has been positioned, a device end (DE) is presented to the channel to indicate that the device has performed its function. The channel executes the next CCW, which contains the SET SECTOR command. A channel end (CE) is presented after the sector address is transferred to the control unit and the channel is free once more for other activity. The control unit instructs the device to issue a sector alert signal when the addressed sector is approaching the head, and when this event happens, a device end (DE) is presented to the channel. The next three CCWs namely, SEARCH ID EQUAL, TRANS-FER IN CHANNEL and READ, cause the channel to be tied up in a loop for searching the record with the given ID and on satisfactory completion of the search, data transfer takes place as indicated by the READ command. Both CE and DE are presented to the channel and the channel, in turn, notifies the CPU by an interruption that the I/O operation is complete.

The main point to note is that the channel is free to perform other I/O activity during seek and rotational delays and that the CPU performs other functions (like executing another program) during the period between device selection and I/O interruption.

1. If a block multiplexer channel is connected to the disk, the channel is available for other operations during seek time and rotational delay; if the channel is not ready when the sector is under the READ/WRITE head, the device tries again after another full revolution.

2. A typical channel program for a disk read has the form:

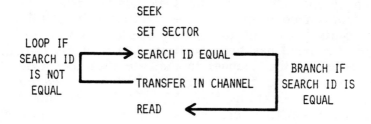

3. The channel and device interaction is shown below:

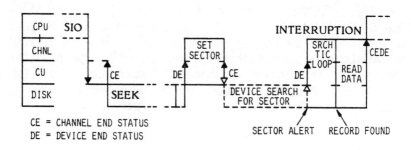

Figure 12-13/CPU, Channel, Control Unit, and Device
Interaction

12.4 EXAMPLES OF DISK DRIVES AND STORAGE CONTROL UNITS

In this section we shall give a few examples of disk drives and storage control units.

IBM 2305 Fixed Head Disk Module and IBM 2835 Storage Control. The IBM 2305 (Model 2) fixed head disk drive module contains six recording disks, with each disk having two data surfaces (there are 12 data surfaces in all). There are 72 tracks per data surface and there is one fixed read/write head (called a recording element) for each track, yielding 72 recording elements for each surface. Figure 12-14 illustrates the arrangement of tracks and recording elements for each surface. As seen from Figure 12-14 there are four access mechanisms, each carrying 18 recording elements. Of the 72 tracks, 64 are used for data recording and 8 are reserved as spares (also called alternate tracks) which are used as substitutes for defective recording tracks.

The 2305 (Model 2) can hold up to 11.25 MB of data and is frequently used as a paging device in a virtual storage operating environment because of its fast access time. Figure 12-15 illustrates the functional capability of the 2305.

The following features are standard for the 2305:

o   sectoring

o   rotational position sensing

The control unit IBM 2835 has the following features:

o   multiple requesting

o   command retry

IBM 3350 Disk Drives and IBM 3830 Storage Control. The IBM 3350 is a disk drive having large capacity and

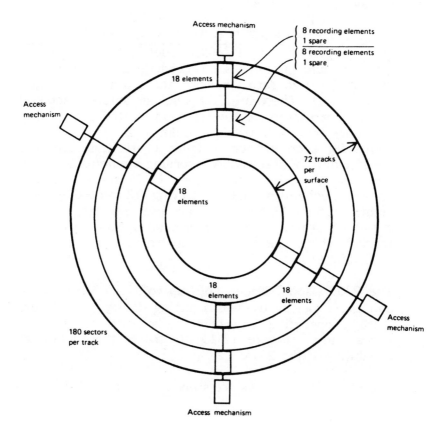

Figure 12-14/Top View of 2305 Model Disk Drive

Number of addressable tracks	768
Bytes per track	14,660
Bytes per module	11,258,880
Rotation time	10 milliseconds
Access time (maximum)	10.25 milliseconds
Access time (average)	5.0 milliseconds
Transfer rate	1.5 MB/sec

Figure 12-15/Capability of IBM 2305 (Model 2) Disk Module

a fast data transfer rate. It is widely used in connection with large-scale data base systems. The 3350 has the following characteristics:

o   It has 16 recording surfaces, one of which is used for servo information, data clocking, rotational position indication and similar control data, plus fixed head storage. The other fifteen recording surfaces are used for user data storage: they are accessible by moving heads and both sides of the surface can be used for data storage.

o   In its native mode, a 3350 unit can store up to 317.5 MB; it has other modes, called compatibility modes, where the disk is not used to its full capacity and is made compatible with the earlier IBM 3330 unit.

o   The 3350 unit (in its native mode) is logically organized into 555 cylinders, each cylinder having 30 tracks. Each track is capable of storing 19,069 bytes; there are 5 cylinders (150 tracks) which are used as alternates, and one cylinder is for reserved use.

o   Each track has a home address, a track descriptor record and one or more data records; each data record has a count area, key area and a data area.

o   A track is selected by its seek address, which is in the form CC HH and normally corresponds to the home address.

o   A record is read from or written to a track, based on an address having the form CC HH R.

o   There are 128 sector marks that divide the surface of the disk into equal areas, and their purpose is to aid in rotational sensing.

CHARACTERISTIC	3350 IN 3330-1 COMPATIBILITY MODE (2 PER DRIVE)	3350 IN 3330-11 COMPATIBILITY MODE	3350 IN NATIVE MODE
CYLINDERS PER DRIVE	404 (PLUS 7 ALTERNATES)	808 (PLUS 7 ALTERNATES)	555 (PLUS 5 ALTERNATES)
TRACKS PER CYLINDER	19	19	30
TRACKS PER DRIVE	7,676 (PLUS 133 ALTERNATES)	13,352 (PLUS 133 ALTERNATES)	16,650 (PLUS 150 ALTERNATES)
TRACK CAPACITY (BYTES)	13,030	13,030	19,069
CYLINDER CAPACITY (BYTES)	247,570	247,570	572,070
DRIVE CAPACITY (APPROX. BYTES)	100 MILLION (PER LOGICAL VOLUME)	200 MILLION	317.5 MILLION

Figure 12-16/Disk Storage Systems

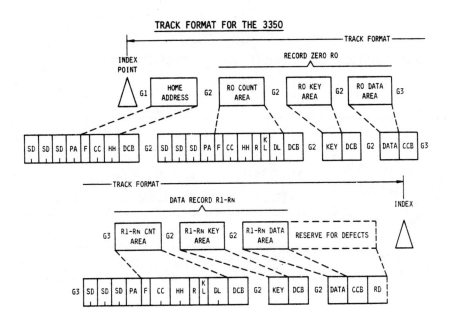

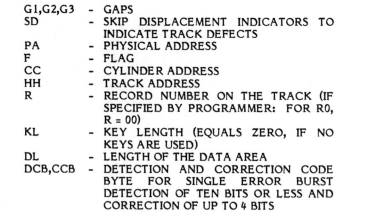

EXPLANATION OF SYMBOLS:

G1,G2,G3	-	GAPS
SD	-	SKIP DISPLACEMENT INDICATORS TO INDICATE TRACK DEFECTS
PA	-	PHYSICAL ADDRESS
F	-	FLAG
CC	-	CYLINDER ADDRESS
HH	-	TRACK ADDRESS
R	-	RECORD NUMBER ON THE TRACK (IF SPECIFIED BY PROGRAMMER: FOR R0, R = 00)
KL	-	KEY LENGTH (EQUALS ZERO, IF NO KEYS ARE USED)
DL	-	LENGTH OF THE DATA AREA
DCB,CCB	-	DETECTION AND CORRECTION CODE BYTE FOR SINGLE ERROR BURST DETECTION OF TEN BITS OR LESS AND CORRECTION OF UP TO 4 BITS

Figure 12-17/Track Format for the 3350

The 3350 units are attached to a channel using a 3830 storage control unit or an Integrated Storage Control (ISC). A maximum of 32 physical drives can be addressed through a single storage control unit. 3350s are usually grouped together in strings. A string can contain up to four dual drives (i.e., two 3350 disk units), and the first unit in each string has a controller if data transfer requirements warrant it, and an alternate controller can be substituted for the last dual drive.

Figure 12-16 illustrates characteristics of the 3350 and Figure 12-17 shows the track and record layout.

13. Miscellaneous Control Units and Devices

As a concluding chapter, we shall briefly describe other control units and devices that are used in IBM computer systems.

IBM 3803/3420 magnetic tape subsystems consist of 3420 magnetic tape drive units that are attached to block multiplexer or selector channels via the 3803 control units. The 3420 tape drive units come in several models that use half-inch nine-track magnetic tapes. (The nine tracks correspond to eight bits plus a parity bit.) The recording density is 1600 bits per inch (BPI) for low speed tapes and 6500 BPI for high speed tapes. Data transfer rates vary from 120 KB/sec (low speed) to 1.25 MB/sec (high speed). The control unit can be connected to a maximum of eight tape units, with restrictions that depend on specific models. Both channel-switching and tape-switching are possible. When channel-switching is used, two channels (both belonging to the same processor or one each from two different processors) can be used to access the same control unit. Tape-switching is analogous to string-switching and permits access of tape drives connected to one control unit by another control unit.

The IBM 3211 printer is a high speed printer capable of printing 2000 lines per minute. It has 132 print positions which can be optionally extended to 150 print positions. The printer can be attached to a byte or block multiplexer channel via the IBM 3811 control unit. The 3811 contains a forms control buffer (FCB) which enables an operator to enter spacing and skipping information pertaining to forms, thus avoiding the use of perforated tapes that have to be manually inserted into the printer to control paper movement as in the case of earlier printers.

The IBM 3505 card reader comes in two models that can read 800 or 1200 cards per minute. It has a micropro grammed control unit that provides buffering capability. The control unit can be attached to a byte or a block multiplexer channel. Data is transferred in byte-interleaved mode when the byte multiplexer channel is used and in the burst mode when the block multiplexer channel is used. The 3505 has the following advantages over earlier card readers:

o   It uses friction feeding instead of picker knives and is therefore less sensitive to frayed edges of cards.

o   It uses a photoelectric read head.

o   It uses automatic feed retries (up to three times) in case of trouble in reading a card.

A 3525 card punch can be attached to the card reader via an adapter that provides completely buffered operation for the card punch.

REFERENCE MATERIAL AND FURTHER READING

o   Interface Specifications

     IBM Manuals

3.1   IBM System/360 and System 370 I/O Interface Channel to Control Unit Original Equipment Manufacturer's Information, GA 22-6974-4

3.2   System/360 I/O Interface Introduction, Student Self-Study Course SR 25-5202-5

o   Data Communications

     IBM Manuals

3.3   Introduction to Advanced Communications Function, GC 30-3033-0

3.4   IBM Synchronous Data Link Control General Information, GA 27-3093-1, 1974

o   Other References

3.5   Communication Architecture for Distributed Systems, R.J. Cypser, Addison Wesley, 1978

3.6   IBM Systems Journal, Volume 15, Number 1, 1978 (This issue contains introductory articles on SNA.)

o   Communications Controller 3705

     IBM Manuals

3.7   IBM 3704 and 3705 Communications Controllers

Principles of Operation, GC 30-3004-5, 1979

3.8   Concepts of IBM 3704 and 3705 Communications Controllers, Student Text, 1979

3.9   IBM 3704 and 3705 Communications Controllers Hardware, Student Text

o   <u>IBM 3270 Information Display System</u>

      IBM Manuals

3.10 "IBM 3270 Operation and Design," Independent Study Program

3.11 "IBM 3270 Information Display System Component Description," GA-27-2749-10, 1980

o   <u>Storage Controls and Disk Drives</u>

      IBM Manuals

3.12 "A Guide to the IBM System/370 Model 158 for System 360 Users," GC 20-1781-1, 1977

3.13 "IBM 3830 Storage Control Model 2," GA 26-1617-5, 1977

3.14 "Reference Manual for IBM 3350," GA 26-1638-2, 1977

o   <u>Miscellaneous Systems</u>

3.15 IBM 8100 Information System, Distributed Office Support Facility, General Information, GC 27-0546-1, 1981

3.16 IBM 3600 Finance Communication System, System Summary, GC-27-0001-8, 1979

APPENDICES

Appendix 1
Concepts Used in Operating Systems

The purpose of this appendix is to provide supplementary material to the text. An understanding of basic concepts used in operating systems implementation is necessary to obtain an appreciation of computer architecture. An operating system is a collection of programs that control the execution of and perform hardware-related functions for application programs. The operating system commonly used with large-scale IBM processors (370/158, 168, 3033, 3081) is IBM's Multiple Virtual Storage (MVS) operating system. In this appendix, we shall use MVS as a framework of our discussion. It is beyond the scope of this text to go into a detailed account of MVS operation and our discussions will be at a simplified level.

1. THE MVS OPERATING SYSTEM

Multiple Virtual Storage (MVS) is the largest and the most complicated operating system designed by a computer manufacturer. It runs on the IBM 370 and 3031, 3032 and 3033 computers and can support multiprocessing (MP) mode of operation. The three most important factors that influenced the design of MVS are the following:

o   virtual storage of up to 16 megabytes for each user

o   tightly coupled multiprocessing

o   sophisticated resource allocation and monitoring facilities

The following is a list of facilities provided by MVS which are of interest from a user's point of view.

Time Sharing Option (TSO). This facility enables a

user to enter, edit, and execute application programs from remote terminals, to browse through and alter catalogs of data sets or contents of program libraries, and perform numerous system functions by privileged users.

Job Entry Subsystems (JES). MVS supports two job entry subsystems (JES2 and JES3) which read jobs into the system, and schedule and manage their execution.

Language Translators. MVS provides a wide variety of language translators, including compilers for COBOL, FORTRAN and PL/1, and an assembler for the basic assembly language (BAL) used by the 370 and 303X series.

Access Methods. MVS provides access methods that are used by application programmers for transfer of data to or from a device or for control of a device. QSAM, BPAM, BDAM, BSAM, ISAM, VSAM, VTAM, TCAM, and BTAM are some of the access methods supported by MVS.

Data Base/Data Communication Systems. MVS supports several data base/data communication systems, the most significant of which are Information Management System (IMS) and Customer Information Control System (CICS).

Measurement Facilities. MVS provides an extensive set of measurement monitors (MF/1, RMF, GTF) for measurement of system performance and system tuning; in addition, MVS has a System Management Facility (SMF) for gathering accounting information and system use information.

Reliability Features. MVS has facilities for improving reliability, availability, and serviceability (RAS) of the system, and has routines for isolating errors and for recovery from software and (where possible) from hardware errors.

In any given installation, many levels of computer personnel interact with MVS. Each level has to be familiar with only that part of MVS which is relevant in carrying out functions assigned to that level. For instance, an application programmer does not have to know the details of execution of his program: how pages are allocated, on which CPU (in a mulitple CPU environment) a task is executed, or the allocation of logical channels to his data set. Application programs are usually written in high level languages (COBOL, PL/1) and the programmer has to be familiar with the job control language (JCL), the commands used in the Time Sharing Option (TSO), and compiling and linkage-editing procedures.

2. BUILDING BLOCKS OF MVS

Figure A-1 illustrates the building blocks of the MVS operating system. The eight blocks shown in the inner circle are the most frequently used components, and they may be regarded as the core of the operating system. The components shown on the outer circle are less frequently used and they can be regarded as the outer shell of the operating system. We shall describe next the functions of each of these components.

2.1 JOB MANAGEMENT

A job is a collection of related programs that are usually executed together. The compilation, link-editing and execution of an application program is an example of a job requiring three job steps, each step consisting of the execution of a distinct program. The functions of job management are listed below:

o   to interpret operator commands (from an operator console) and to route appropriate messages.

o   to read job input data and to write job output data from peripheral devices.

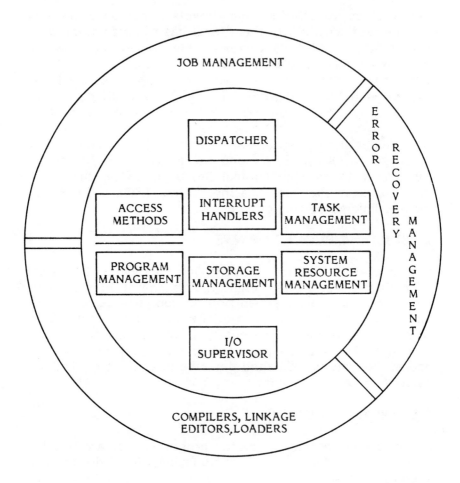

FIGURE A-1/A Simplified View of Building Blocks
of the MVS Operating System

o   to allocate I/O devices to a job and to notify the operator of the physical data units (e.g., tape reel, disk pack, etc.) that have to be mounted prior to the execution of a job.

o   to convert the job into tasks that can be processed by task management.

Under MVS a program can be executed in a variety of ways: the master console operator can start a program by typing the START command, a TSO user can start a program by the LOGON command, or a deck of program cards can be submitted via a card reader. An address space of 16 MB is created for a started program and for a program logged on from a TSO terminal. In the case of jobs that are submitted via local or remote card readers, or those that are created by user programs, a new address space is not created for each job entering the system. In Figure A-2, we show the sequence of operations in the case of jobs entered in this manner. A job entry subsystem (JES2, JES3) breaks down the job stream into job control language (JCL) statements and input data. A program called a Converter processes the JCL into intermediate text. Control blocks are created in the Scheduler Work Area (SWA), and the JCL text is further processed by an Interpreter which creates and chains tables in the SWA. The job entry system is executed again, and an "initiator" is assigned to the job. In this context, the function of the initiator is to execute each job step as a task in the initiator's address space (a certain number of initiators are specified at system definition time). The initiator is a program that creates a new task for each job step, in the case of job entry as shown in Figure A-2. In the case of a started task or a task which is logged on from the TSO terminal, the initiator's address space is not used for running the task and the initiator returns after performing various control functions.

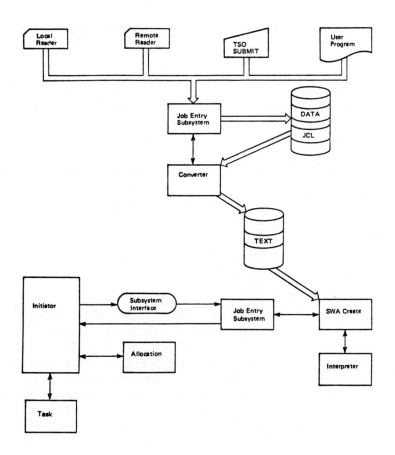

Figure A-2/Job Entry

2.2 TASK MANAGEMENT

A task is a unit of work that is executed by the dispatcher. A job step can be regarded as a task. A task can create another task and also activate or suspend a task created by it. The functions of the task management are listed below:

o   creation and deletion of tasks

o   control of execution of tasks by changing priorities

o   enqueing (dequeuing) tasks to (from) serially reusable resources.

o   synchronization of events by using event control operations like WAIT and POST.

Creation and Deletion of Subtasks. Normally, a task is created by the job entry system for a job step. A program executing as a task can create a new task by using the ATTACH macro instruction. A newly created task can compete for system resources with other tasks.

The deletion of a task is done by means of the DETACH macro instruction which frees up resources used by the task and performs clean-up functions.

Enqueing and Dequeuing. A resource, in the sense that it is used here, is any entity that is necessary for the execution of a computer program. Thus, resource can denote memory, CPU, channel, device, or another computer program.

A serially reusable resource is a resource that can be used by only one user at a time and is capable of reusage. A device is serially reusable and so is a page frame in memory. A program is serially reusable if it restores data and code that is modified during its execution to their status before execution; in other words, a serially reusable program either initializes itself at the start of execution or performs clean-up operations at the end of the program so that it can be executed again. Many transaction-handling application programs are designed to be serially reusable so that the copy of the code existing in main storage can be used repeatedly and thus fetching programs from auxiliary storage can be avoided.

A queue of users is associated with a serially reusable resource. If the resource is "busy" (i.e., it is servicing a user) a user is made to wait in a queue until such time that the resource is available.

ENQ, DEQ and RESERVE macro instructions are used by operating system modules to control the allocation and de-allocation of serially reusable resources. The resource may be a data set, a record within a data set, a program or work areas within main storage. Associated with the resource is a queue control block (QCB) and queue elements pertaining to requests. The QCB indicates whether or not the resource is busy (i.e., another program is using the resource) and if it is, a queue element is created for the current request and the requesting program is put in a wait state. If the resource is not in use, a queue element is created and the resource is marked busy; control is returned to the calling program. RESERVE is used in conjunction with shared DASD to obtain exclusive control of a device. The de-allocation of resources is done via the DEQ macro, which removes the appropriate queue element and notifies a waiting task by means of POST macro that the resource is available.

Synchronization of Events. An event is an end result or a postulated outcome whose occurrence triggers a set of specified responses. Examples of events are completion of an I/O activity, the expiration of a time interval, or the termination of the execution of a certain program. In a formal sense, an event can be synchronized by two operations that are associated with it, namely WAIT and POST. A WAIT is issued against an event to indicate that no further activity by the program can take place until the occurrence of the event. A POST is issued to denote the occurrence of the event and the subsequent re-activation of the program.

An event control block (ECB) is used to denote the status of an event and to store control information pertaining to an event. A common use of the event control block is to deactivate or activate a task in a multiprogramming environment.

Let us assume that a task is waiting for an I/O operation to take place. An ECB with a wait flag can be used to indicate the waiting status of the task. When the I/O operation is complete the ECB can be posted to indicate event completion. Figure A-3 shows a simplified ECB and the setting and resetting of flags by WAIT and POST activities.

2.3 PROGRAM MANAGEMENT

The functions of program management are the following:

o   Loading program modules

o   Transferring control from one module to another

o   Synchronizing the execution of modules

An MVS module or user program issues a LINK, LOAD, XCTL, SYNCH macro which is processed by Program Management.

The LINK macro is used by one program module to invoke another program module with the intention of gaining control from the second program module after termination of its execution; XCTL is used with the intention of relinquishing control to the invoked program. Figure A-4 shows the flow of control between program modules as a result of LINK and XCTL instructions.

This is a good place to explain the various phases of creation of a program module, starting with a program

written in assembler or a high-level language and ending
with a program module that can be executed by the
computer.   A language translator accepts as input a
program in a high level language; the statements in the
program are called source statements and the program
itself is called a source module. The language translator
creates an object module from the source module; the
object module consists of machine language instructions in
a nonexecutable format. Before they can be executed, the
modules have to be processed by (i) the linkage editor and
(ii) Program Fetch. The linkage editor converts one or
more object module(s) into a load module, which is stored
in a program library (in auxiliary storage) specified by the
user. The linkage editor is not invoked by MVS routines
but is executed as a job step by the user. Program Fetch is
an MVS routine that is called by Program Management
routines such as LOAD. The load module created by the
linkage editor uses consecutive addresses starting from
zero upwards. Program Fetch assigns consecutive virtual
addresses to the load module, starting from a specific
virtual address.

Program Fetch has its own channel programs that transfer
the module from auxiliary storage to real storage at
first: before issuing a Start I/O, pages are fixed to receive
records from the module text from auxiliary storage. It
then replaces the addresses in the load module with virtual
storage addresses, as explained earlier.

The LOAD macro is used for program fetching only, and
can be used before the LINK or XCTL macro.

The SYNCH macro is used by MVS modules to give temporary control to another program (not necessarily running
in the supervisor state) with the intention of obtaining
control back after the execution of the second program; in
order to use SYNCH, the second program must be in virtual storage.

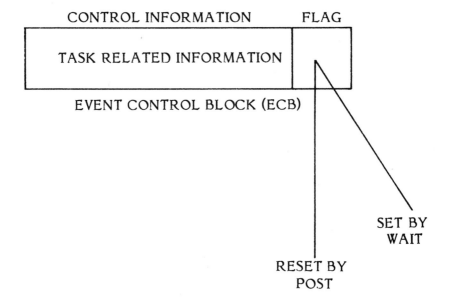

Figure A-3/Event Control Block Operation

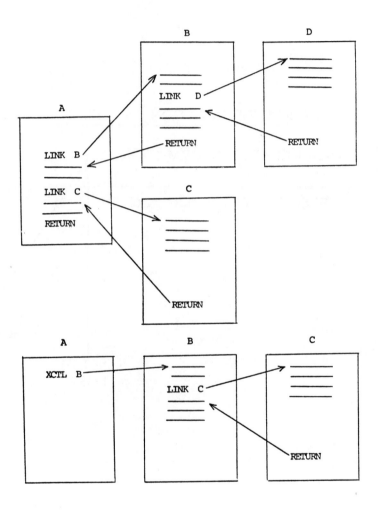

Figure A-4/Flow of Control Using Link
and XCTL Instructions

2.4 DISPATCHER

Multiprogramming (also known as multitasking) denotes the overlapping and interleaving of the execution of several application programs in order to effectively utilize the resources of the computer system and is usually accomplished by executing one program while another program is waiting for completion of an I/O operation. Central to the concept of multiprogramming is a certain view of application program behavior which we shall explain next.

A program has two sets of instructions, one set using the CPU and the other set the channel. These two instruction sets are interspersed throughout the body of the program. For instance, a program performs logical and arithmetical functions (using only the CPU) for a certain time interval and then issues a request for reading to or writing from a peripheral device. The program usually is written in such a manner that the requested I/O operation has to be completed before it can proceed to use the CPU again. Thus, program behavior consists of the following events:

o   using the CPU

o   initiating an I/O operation

o   waiting for completion of an I/O operation

The duration of an I/O operation is significantly longer than the duration of CPU usage. For instance, it may take 40 miliseconds to perform a disk I/O operation and it may take several seconds for an operator to enter data from a terminal. The average instruction execution is of the order of, say, 1 microsecond on several medium and large scale computers. Hence, 40,000 CPU instructions can be executed during the time it takes to complete a disk I/O; this figure gets into the range of millions when an I/O involves a terminal operator.

Figure A-5 shows the alternating sequence of CPU operations and I/O operations during program execution. During CPU operation, the CPU is not available to any other program. During I/O execution, the CPU is available to other programs but the device involved in the I/O operation is not available to any other program. The channel (as long as it is not a selector channel) is available to other programs for performing I/O operations.

Under multiprogramming, when the CPU is available during the execution of a program, another program is allowed to use it. Figure A-5 shows the sequence of activities in a multiprogramming environment. Assume that three programs A, B and C (having priorities in the named order) are to be executed. At time zero, program A starts execution. It starts an I/O operation at t_1, and the CPU is given to program B, which executes instructions until t_2 when it starts an I/O operation. C starts executing until t_3 when it is interrupted by the completed I/O operation performed by A. Since C has a lower priority than A, it is put in a "waiting for execution" state and A is given control of the CPU. A is interrupted at t_4 by B's completed I/O operation and resumes its execution because it has higher priority than B. B is put in a "waiting for execution" state. At t_5 A starts an I/O operation and the CPU is available to the two waiting programs B and C. B is given control because it has higher priority and performs CPU operations until t_6 when it starts an I/O operation and control is given to program C.

The dispatcher can be regarded as the manager of the CPU. Its function is to scan a queue of tasks within an address space that has the highest priority among several competing address spaces, and to give control to the task having the highest priority. The control is given by loading Control Registers 0 and 1 with page size and segment table address (to enable dynamic address translation for that address space to proceed) and the Program Status Word with the next instruction address to be used by the task. If the task queue for every address space is empty, the dispatcher puts the CPU into a hardware waiting condition.

Once a task gains control of the CPU, it monopolizes the CPU until an interruption is received by the CPU. The interruption can be due to an SVC issued by the task itself

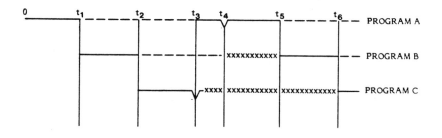

LEGEND: ———— CPU OPERATION

—— I/O OPERATION

∨ INTERRUPT

xxxxxx WAITING FOR EXECUTION STATE

Figure A-5/Multiprogramming Activity Sequence

during its course of execution, by the completion of an I/O event pertaining to some other task, or by various exception conditions. After the interruption handler services the interruption, control is returned to the dispatcher which saves the status of the interrupted program and scans the task queue as mentioned earlier.

In addition to tasks, MVS has other dispatchable entities known as Service Request Blocks (SRBs) and Asynchronous Exits. We shall not go into details regarding these here.

2.5 INTERRUPTION HANDLERS

An interruption handler is given control by the address in the new PSW whenever an interruption occurs, and the following interruption handlers are used by MVS.

o   SVC Interruption Handler

o   I/O Interruption Handler

o   External Interruption Handler

o   Program Check Interruption Handler

o   Machine Check Interruption Handler

o   Restart Interruption Handler

The following functions are usually performed by the interruption handlers.

Saving the Environment. The environment usually denotes the set of registers used by a program and the Program Status Word. Saving the environment means storing the registers and the Program Status Word.

Disabling Other Interruptions. The CPU is in an enabled state when it is ready to accept interruptions, and it is in a disabled state when interruptions are not accepted. Certain interruption handling routines run in a disabled state because of the nature of the functions performed by them.

Passing Control to Appropriate Routine. Using the indicators stored by hardware, the interruption handling routine identifies the cause of interruption and branches to an operating system routine for taking further action. Thus, the SVC interruption handler invokes routines to handle SVCs based on the number (0 to 255) that identifies the type of SVC instruction; likewise, the I/O interruption handler passes control to the I/O supervisor to analyze the cause of the interruption and to perform steps to process the interruption.

2.6 STORAGE MANAGEMENT

These routines manage real, virtual, and auxiliary storage and perform allocation and deallocation of pages, page frames, and slots.

2.6.1 MVS Storage Organization

Three types of storage are used by the operating system, namely real storage, virtual storage and auxiliary storage. Real storage is divided into 4K byte page frames, auxiliary storage into 4K byte page slots, and virtual storage into 64K byte segments and within a segment, into 4K pages. A virtual address using a 24-bit addressing scheme comprises a segment index, page index, and byte displacement as explained in Part I of the text.

Under MVS, 16 MB of virtual storage, resulting from the 24-bit addressing scheme, is available to each address space. One or more tasks can be executed within this address space.

2.6.1.1 Virtual Storage Layout

The address space of 16MB comprises system areas as well as private areas. A map of virtual storage layout is given in Figure A-6. The system areas are the nucleus, common service area, pageable link pack area and system queue area. The system areas are shared by all address spaces and can be regarded as global areas that are common. The address space's private area is used exclusively for the execution of tasks within the address space and comprises a scheduler work area, local system queue area in addition to the tasks' working areas.

Nucleus. The nucleus is always resident in main storage and starts at location 0 (except in the case of tightly coupled MP systems which are discussed in Part I). The first 4K bytes of real storage is used by a table called Prefixed Storage Area (PSA) which contains system related information and pointers to other system tables. The PSA contains the following types of information.

- Old PSWs

- New PSWs

- Channel Status Word

- Channel Address Word

In addition to the PSA, the nucleus contains page frame tables and various routines that constitute the resident part of the MVS operating system.

Common Service Area (CSA). The CSA is used for data that is common to several address spaces. For instance, Information Management System (IMS) keeps several data base management routines and data base buffers in the CSA so that they can be shared by several IMS address spaces. The buffers used by Job Entry Systems are also kept in the CSA.

Pageable Link Pack Area (PLPA). The PLPA is used to hold SVC routines, access methods and other system programs that are shared by all users of the system. An installation's routines, to be shared by all users, can also be placed in the PLPA.

System Queue Area (SQA). The SQA contains tables and queues relating to the entire system. Several control blocks and queues used by various MVS modules are kept in this area, including page tables pertaining to CSA and SQA. SQA also contains information relating to address spaces.

Scheduler Work Area (SWA). The SWA contains tables and control blocks pertaining to an address space, created at the time of scheduling a job.

Local System Queue Area (LSQA). The LSQA contains tables and queues that are used for local tasks associated with the control and execution of address spaces.

2.6.1.2 Virtual Storage Operations

The internal addresses used by the program are virtual addresses and they are converted to real addresses at program execution time by the Dynamic Address Translation (DAT) hardware. DAT computes a 24-bit real address from a 24-bit virtual address using the scheme explained in Part I.

For each address space that is in operation within the system, segment tables and page tables are created by MVS during initialization of the address space.

The segment table contains addresses of page tables pertaining to segments and each entry indicates the length of the page table and its address. A page table contains an entry of page addresses within the segment. Control Register 1 contains the segment table address for the executing address space.

Page Operations: During translation, if a page is not in real storage as indicated by a bit in the page table entry, a page translation exception (or page fault) interruption takes place. A page-in is the transfer of a page from a page slot in auxiliary storage to a page frame in real storage. Associated with the page table there is another table called the external page table which gives the slot location for the page. A page fault exception causes a page-in operation by the system.

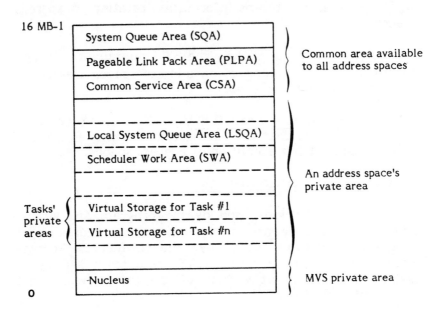

Figure A-6/Virtual Storage Layout of Each
16MB Address Space Under MVS

The operating system steals pages from address spaces on a least referenced usage basis if the total number of pages allocated to all address spaces reaches a certain threshold. When a page is thus stolen, it may have been modified by an address space in which case it is written out to auxiliary storage. This process is known as page-out; in other words, the transfer of a page from a page frame in real storage to a page slot in auxiliary storage is called a page-out. Sometimes a page is written out to two external storage devices for reasons of data security; this procedure is called page duplexing.

A page is called fixed if its page frame cannot be stolen from the address space. A long term page fix lasts through the duration of the program; many system tasks and communication monitors fix pages this way. A short term page fix denotes fixing a page frame for a short duration; for instance, prior to the start of an I/O operation, pages pertaining to the data buffer are fixed and they are released after completion of the I/O operation.

A page is reclaimed if a page frame that has been stolen from an address space is reassigned to it in such a way that the previous slot/frame mapping is maintained.

Swap Operations: An address space is swapped in if pages necessary for its execution are transferred all at once from auxiliary storage to real storage; it is swapped out if all its pages in real storage are transferred to auxiliary storage. Swapping is used as a means of allocating real storage to address spaces.

Summary of Operations: The virtual storage operations that are performed by MVS are the following:

- creating or deleting virtual storage control blocks for address spaces.

- creating or freeing virtual storage for address spaces.

- maintaining tables that establish correspondences between (a) virtual pages and auxiliary storage seek addresses and, (b) virtual pages and real page frames.

- processing page faults in conjunction with the I/O Supervisor which performs the actual I/O operation on the auxiliary storage device.

- page stealing in conjunction with the System Resource Manager (SRM).

- swapping address spaces in conjunction with the System Resource Manager (SRM).

2.6.1.3 Real Storage Organization.

The total available real storage is dependent on the system; in the case of the IBM 370/168 (model 3), 8MB is the maximum available real storage.

Not all of real storage is available for usage by application programs. For instance, the nucleus and the SQA are resident in real storage and access methods like VTAM and TCAM need a certain amount of fixed pages. It is not unusual for large installations to have 2 to 3 MB of real storage used exclusively for system use.

Real storage organization consists of maintaining queues of page frames and the status of page frames. We shall discuss these in the paragraph on MVS Storage Management Modules.

2.6.1.4 Auxiliary Storage Organization

Auxiliary storage exists physically as paging data sets in a direct access storage device. There are paging data sets for system areas as well for user's private areas. IBM 2305 (models 1 and 2) fixed head devices and IBM 3350 movable head devices are commonly used for defining paging data sets. The data sets are organized according to 4K byte blocks for page-slots. Page-slots in auxiliary storage are given Logical Slot IDs (LSIDs) which have seek addresses corresponding to them. The mapping between LSIDs and seek addresses is maintained by tables used by the

Auxiliary Storage Manager (ASM).

2.6.2 MVS Storage Management Modules

MVS has three storage management modules, namely, Real Storage Manager (RSM), Virtual Storage Manager (VSM), and Auxiliary Storage Manager (ASM). There is a fair amount of overlap between these routines and initially we shall try to describe their methods of operation on an individual basis; subsequently, we shall show how several storage operations are performed by the combined action of all three modules.

2.6.2.1 Virtual Storage Manager (VSM)

Virtual Storage Management consists primarily of the allocation and deallocation of virtual storage. We have seen that certain virtual storage areas are sharable by address spaces within the system and by tasks within an address space. The size and address of global virtual storage areas (e.g., CSA, SQA, etc.) that are shared by all address spaces are defined at system generation.

The following concepts are used in allocation and deallocation of virtual storage:

o   virtual storage is divided into 256 subpools, with numbers assigned from 0 to 255; the subpools are allocated to the global and local areas of virtual storage and the subpool numbers are used as parameters in the storage allocation and deallocation routines (GETMAIN and FREEMAIN).

o   virtual storage is assigned in blocks within a subpool or "quick cells" within a subpool; the blocks are 4K in size and the quick cells are small fixed length storage blocks in the SQA or LSQA.

o   virtual storage blocks do not have any tangible existence and are represented by control blocks which are used for virtual storage bookkeeping purposes to ensure that shared and non-shared virtual storage areas are properly assigned to address spaces and tasks.

A GETMAIN macro is used for allocation of virtual storage and a FREEMAIN macro is used for deallocation of virtual storage by application programs and system programs. These macro instructions result in SVC interruptions that pass control to VSM routines. The GETMAIN processing tries to find storage from an existing virtual storage block and if it is not found, creates a new block.

For system use, the GETCELL and FREECELL routines obtain small fixed-length blocks of storage in the SQA and LSQA. They are not available to the application programmer.

The main routines of the Virtual Storage Manager perform the following functions:

o   Initialize an address space in conjunction with Real Storage Manager.

o   Perform GETMAIN and FREEMAIN functions.

o   Perform GETCEL and FREECELL functions.

o   Perform clean-up functions after task and address space termination.

2.6.2.2 Real Storage Manager (RSM)

Real Storage Management consists of maintaining queues of page frames, fixing and releasing pages, stealing pages and initiating page fault operations. The page frame queues are maintained on a basis of usage with the least referenced frame always at the top of the queue. There are page frame queues for global system areas as well as for local user areas.

Each time a page is modified, a hardware reference bit is turned on and when that page is stolen it is paged out. A logical slot identification number (LSID) is given to the page and this LSID is entered in the external page reference table.

The Page Frame Table has an entry for every page frame in real storage. Each entry contains the following information:

o   ID of the address space that uses the page frame.

o   segment numbers and page number of the virtual page.

o   status of the page frame (in use or available for use).

o   unreferenced interval count.

Before we explain what the unreferenced interval count means, two flags that are set by hardware pertaining to reading from a frame and writing to a frame should be described. Associated with every page-frame, there is a reference bit and a change bit which are set by hardware. The reference bit is on when a page-frame is referenced (i.e., a real storage access for reading or writing takes place); the change bit is on when the contents of a page-frame are changed (i.e., a memory location within the page-frame is accessed for writing). These bits are not part of the page-frame table entry but are contained in the storage protect key for each 2K block of storage maintained by hardware as explained in Part I of this book. The unreference interval count (UIC) indicates the time during which a page has gone unreferenced and is set by the Real Storage Manager at periodic intervals as a result of requests from the System Resources Manager (SRM).

RSM's functions are briefly described below:

o   initializing segment and page table entries.

o   assigning a real frame to a virtual page during page-fault processing, which is described later.

o   fixing pages in real storage and releasing such pages.

o   taking the initial steps for transferring a page to virtual storage (i.e., paging out).

o   stealing pages in conjunction with SRM, as described next.

Page Stealing and Paging Out.   Page frames are stolen from address spaces when there is a scarcity of page frames.   The criterion for page stealing is the unreferenced interval count (UIC) of the page frame which reflects the number of intervals during which the frame was not referenced.   The System Resources Manager (SRM) sets the page stealing operation in motion when the number of available frames drops beyond a certain threshold and passes to the Real Storage Manager a parameter list indicating the type of page to be stolen (e.g., page belonging to CSA, local page, etc.), an address space list, and the UIC.   The UIC is stored in the Page Frame Table Entry and is updated by RSM at periodic intervals by examining the hardware page reference bit for each page on the local and common queus, on request by SRM.

The steal routines of RSM scan the page frame table entries of local and common frames (which are queued from high UIC to low UIC) and select a number of pages (as specified by SRM) as candidates for stealing. If a page that is a candidate for stealing has not been modified in any way, it is placed in the available frame queue; if it has been modified, it is paged out.

Page Fault Processing.   A page fault occurs during the course of program execution when DAT fails to find a page frame entry in the Page Table for a virtual page used by the program.   This is also known as a page translation exception and causes a program interruption.   Control is passed by the interruption handler to RSM for allocating a page frame and this is done normally by assigning the first frame from the available frame queue.   The Auxiliary Storage Manager processes the page fault request at this stage and it gives the seek address of the slot and other necessary information to I/O Supervisor, which performs a

Start I/O operation.

The program that gave rise to the page fault is suspended by the interruption handler while the page-in operation takes place and other dispatchable work is executed by the dispatcher in the interim.

2.6.2.3 Auxiliary Storage Manager

Auxiliary Storage Management consists of maintaining tables for obtaining seek addresses from LSIDs, creating paging channel programs, coordinating with the I/O Supervisor in starting a page I/O operation and retaking control from I/O Supervisor after completion of the I/O operation.

2.7 SYSTEM RESOURCES MANAGER (SRM)

The System Resources Manager (SRM) gives the MVS operating system a degree of sophistication that is unique to it, since other large scale operating systems do not have any resource management modules that can match the functions performed by SRM.

In a broad sense the function of SRM is the allocation of resources among address spaces. A resource denotes CPU, real memory and I/O channels. In performing this function, SRM accumulates statistics pertaining to utilization of CPU, channel, frame, slot and several such items. Thus, in a narrower sense, the functions of SRM can be described as performance optimization within constraints set by the installation and performance monitoring in the dynamic environment of address space execution.

The strategies used by SRM to achieve optimal resource allocation are summarized as follows:

o Real storage management -- pages are stolen from address spaces when there are shortages, and address spaces are swapped in and out under certain conditions.

o   CPU management -- dispatching priorities are recom-
    puted for certain classes of users, and address spaces
    are swapped in and out under certain conditions.

o   I/O management -- load balancing is performed on
    logical channels, and address spaces are swapped out
    under certain conditions.

SRM has a set of parameters that can be assigned values
by the installation to improve performance.

SRM views each address space as having the following
properties:

-   it belongs to a domain.

-   it has a dispatching priority.

-   it has installation performance specifications.

A domain is a set of one or more address spaces. A domain
has the following properties:

-   it has a minimum multiprogramming level, i.e., the
    minimum number of address spaces that should be
    guaranteed access to the system's resources at any
    given instant of time.

-   it has a maximum multiprogramming level, i.e., the
    maximum number of address spaces that are permitted
    access to the system's resources.

-   it has a weighting factor that expresses the relative
    weight (importance) of a given domain compared to
    other domains.

The term service is defined as a linear combination of CPU
service units (i.e., CPU execution time), I/O service units
(i.e., sum of I/O counts for the address space) and storage
service units (i.e., real page frame multiplied by CPU
service units). The fomula for service is given as:

SERVICE = CPU * CPU SERVICE UNITS + IOC * I/O

SERVICE UNITS + MSO * STORAGE SERVICE UNITS

where CPU, IOC, and MSO are coefficients that vary according to the installation.

Service rate is defined as the service consumed by an address space during a given time interval in which the address space is active, divided by the duration of the time interval. For the calculation of the service rate, both service and time are set to zero when the address space is swapped in; also, when an address space is swapped out, time is again reset to zero and service remains at its prior value.

A performance objective is a function that expresses a relationship between the service rate for an address space and the workload level. The graph of a performance objective is given in Figure A-7 (a). The workload level varies from 1 to 100. The workload level is used as a recommendation value for swapping address spaces belonging to the same domain. In Figure A-7(b) we show two address spaces, A and B, having performance objectives P and P . The service rates are S and S and the corresponding workload levels are W and W . The address space with the smaller workload level or recommendation value (B, in our example) is a candidate for being swapped out, taking into account other criteria such as the minimum multiprogramming level for the domain.

The performance objective for each address space is specified by an installation, as part of the MVS system definition. As mentioned, the operating system uses the performance objective in making swap recommendations for address space within a domain.

Dispatching priority denotes the priority assigned to an address space for dispatching purposes. Ready address spaces with the highest priority are dispatched first. The range of dispatching priority is from 0 through 255. This

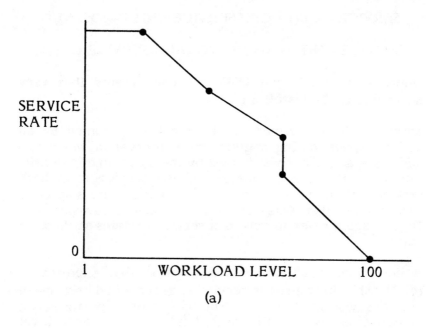

(a)

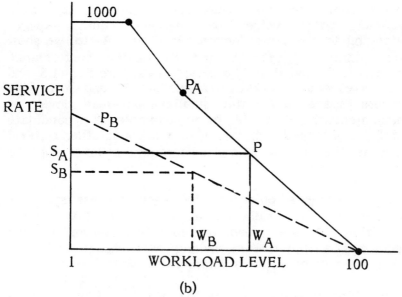

(b)

Figure A-7/Service Rates and Workload Levels

range is divided into 16 sets with 16 priorities per set. One of these sets is called the Automatic Priority Group (APG). SRM adjusts the dispatching priorities of all address spaces that are assigned APG by the installation.

SRM Method of Operation. A large number of SRM modules are timer-driven, meaning that they are invoked at prespecified time intervals. SRM makes use of the timer supervision facilities of MVS to schedule various algorithms at specified intervals. When an interval expires and a timer interruption occurs, the interruption handler notifies SRM via a TIMEREXP SYSEVENT. A SYSEVENT is a macro instruction used by MVS modules to communicate with SRM, and the TIMEREXP is one of such SYSEVENTS. Control is given to SRM's module in charge of periodic scheduling of algorithms and it schedules the following algorithms if they are due for scheduling:

- compute logical channel utilization.

- compute CPU utlization.

- recompute dispatching priorities for those using APG.

- compute highest UIC and adjust invocation interval.

- check for auxiliary storage shortage.

- compute work load for address spaces.

- perform swap analysis.

In addition to the timer-driven algorithms, SRM executes two other sets of routines called deferred algorithms and deferred actions. The deferred algorithms are those SRM algorithms that are scheduled on request from other modules of MVS (e.g., RSM). The following are deferred algorithms:

- Real Page Shortage Prevention

- Page Steal Criteria Establishment

These are invoked via a SYSEVENT called AVQLOW which is issued by RSM when the number of available page frames has fallen below a threshold established at system generation time.

Deferred actions are those requested by an address space or by SRM itself on behalf of an address space. Examples of deferred actions are the following:

- move an address space from the wait queue to the out queue.

- set new Installation Performance Specifications (IPS).

SRM Algorithms. We shall briefly describe the functions of the various algorithms that are used by SRM for data gathering and control purposes.

The data gathering algorithms used by SRM are the following:

- An algorithm that computes the CPU utilization using the formula:

UTILIZATION =

$$100 - \frac{\text{(Sum of wait times on each CPU)}*100}{\text{(Elapsed time since last entry)}*\text{Number of CPUs}}$$

The wait time for each CPU is obtained from a system table which contains the time during which the CPU was in wait state.

- An algorithm that computes the logical channel utilization (i.e., the percentage of recent I/O requests that encountered a busy condition), the logical channel request rate (rate of recent I/O requests per second) and the logical channel utilization factor (the square of the difference between a threshold utilization and actual utilization, with a sign indicating whether the channel is overutilized or under utilized.)

- An algorithm for obtaining the highest unreferenced interval count (UIC) for all page frames (done in conjunction with RSM); this highest UIC is used as a criterion for stealing pages when a shortage exists.

- An algorithm to calculate the service accumulated by an address space and to compute the workload level at which it is receiving service and to set a recommendation value (RV) which is numerically equivalent to the workload level.

The control algorithms used by SRM are the following:

- An algorithm to halve or double the invocation interval of the routine that calculates the highest UIC, the idea being that the interval is progressively halved if there is an acute shortage of real frames.

- An algorithm to swap out an address space belonging to a domain that has multiple address space. Each domain has an entry in the domain descriptor table (DMDT) pertaining to it. The DMDT is searched to see if a domain has a multiprogramming level (MPL) higher than its target value; in such a case the user with the lowest recommendation value (RV) is swapped out.

- An algorithm to swap in an address space that has been swapped out before, by seeing if the domain's MPL is less than its target and swapping in the address space having the highest RV.

2.8 ACCESS METHODS

An application program usually employs an access method in performing an I/O operation. An access method is an interface between an application program and the I/O Supervisor; access methods are provided by the operating system and they relieve the application program from the burden of writing channel programs, building various control blocks required by the I/O Supervisor and handling termination conditions. Examples of access methods are

Basic Telecommunication Access Method (BTAM), Virtual
Storage Access Method (VSAM) and Basic Partitioned
Access Method (BPAM). The earlier access methods used
by the operating system for the IBM 360, and which are
incorporated in MVS, fall under the categories of queued
and basic. Queued access methods primarily apply to
sequential data organizations and are used by GET and
PUT macro instructions. Basic access methods apply to
nonsequential data operations and are used by READ and
WRITE macro instructions. We shall briefly describe
commonly used data organization techniques and the
access methods that are used with such techniques.

Sequential Organization. Data records are stored and
retrieved sequentially (as in a tape) and the access methods used in this context are Queued Sequential Access
Method (QSAM) and Basic Sequential Access Method
(BSAM). QSAM handles the blocking and de-blocking of
physical records. A physical record is defined as a block of
logical records and QSAM stores and retrieves logical
records. QSAM manages buffers that hold logical records
and buffers are written out to a physical device by QSAM
only when they are full. GET and PUT macro instructions
are used by the application program in conjunction with
QSAM. BSAM, on the other hand, only initiates I/O operations and it is up to the application program to test for I/O
completion and perform all operations after completion.
READ and WRITE macro instructions are used by the
application program to retrieve or store records in conjunction with BSAM.

Indexed Sequential Organization. Records are kept on
direct storage devices according to keys specified in the
record. A set of indexes are maintained by the access
method to facilitate retrieval of data by key. There are
several access methods that can be used with indexed
sequential organization and we shall describe only one such
method, namely Virtual Storage Access Method (VSAM).
VSAM stores records in blocks having fixed length, called
control intervals. Control intervals are grouped together
in control areas. The physical organization of data according to tracks within cylinders is replaced in VSAM with the

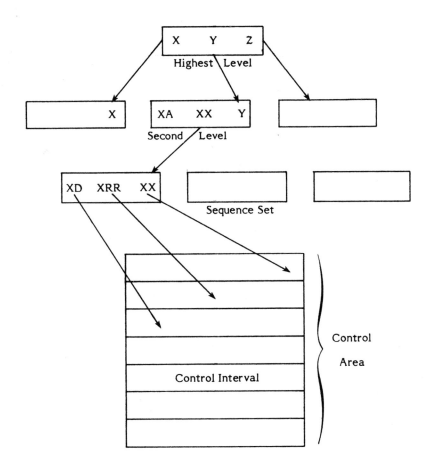

Figure A-8/3-Level VSAM Index Structure

logical organization or data in control intervals within control areas. A control interval may be part of a track or span tracks; likewise a control area may be part of a cylinder or span cylinders (VSAM's predecessor, known as Indexed Sequential Access Method (ISAM) provided a track/cylinder framework of data organization). VSAM maintains several index levels. The purpose of the indexes is to obtain the control interval address for a particular key. ISAM used a master index, a cylinder index and a track index to arrive at the location of a record having a specified key. In the case of VSAM, the highest level index is contained in one single control interval. The lowest level contains several control intervals and each control interval addresses a control area. The intermediate levels contain control intervals that are addressed by higher levels, as illustrated in Figure A-8. The lowest level control intervals are called sequence sets. We cannot go into details regarding VSAM operation or the specification of parameters for VSAM data sets. We shall, however, mention some of the unique characteristics of VSAM, namely:

a. , A data set can be sequenced (a) on the basis of a key, in which case it is called a key sequenced data set (KSDS), (b) on the basis of the sequential order in which records are loaded, in which case it is called an entry sequenced data set (ESDS) or, (c) on the basis of relative record numbers, in which case it is called a relative record data set; a VSAM data set is called a cluster.

b. When a cluster is defined, distributed free space in each control interval can be allocated for future insertions.

c. New records are inserted in the free space in the control interval and if there is not sufficient free space, the contorl interval is split into two control intervals (i.e., a new control interval is created in addition to the old one). This technique for insertion is to be contrasted with the one used in ISAM whereby insertions are placed into an overflow areas and chained together.

Direct Organization.   Records are stored on a direct access storage device and are retrieved and stored in a non-sequential manner.   Basic Direct Access Method (BDAM) is the access method used with the direct organization and the application program issues READ and WRITE macros which only initiate I/O operations and return control to the application program before I/O completion. Hence, the user has to test for the completion of the I/O operation himself.

Partitioned Organization.   This method is used to store programs, procedures, and related material.   Under this organization, a data set, on a direct access storage device, consists of members.   A member may be a program or a job control language procedure, for instance.   Each partitioned data set has a directory of members.   Physically, a member consists of a number of sequentially organized records.   Basic Partitioned Access Method (BPAM) is the access method used in conjunction with this organization. BPAM maintains the directoy and accesses members listed in the directory; the records within the member are read sequentially using BSAM or QSAM.

Telecommunication Access Methods

The telecommunication access methods supported by MVS are Basic Telecommunications Access Method (BTAM), Telecommunications Access Method (TCAM), and Virtual Telecommunications Access Method (VTAM).   Here we shall describe VTAM since it is the latest of the three telecommunications access methods.

VTAM was announced by IBM in 1971 as an alternative to the existing communication methods, namely BTAM and TCAM.

The early design objectives of VTAM were the following:

o   Sharing of Communication Resources

o   Utilization of 3705 Communications Controllers

o   Distributing Network Control Functions

o   Supporting Full-Duplex Line Protocols

o   Supporting Programmable Device Controllers

Sharing of communication resources means that a line or a remote terminal should be available for multiple users accessing more than one program. Under BTAM, lines and terminals are dedicated to a particular application (e.g., CICS, IMS) and sharing of resources between two programs is not possible. Under VTAM, application programs acquire resources as and when they need them and release the resources when they are no longer needed.

VTAM uses the programmable capability of the IBM 3705 communications controllers and interacts with the network control program (NCP) residing in the IBM 3705. Under VTAM, line handling and recovery functions (plus several other functions) are done by the 3705. On the other hand, under BTAM, the lines and terminals were meant to be connected to the host via a Transmission Control Unit (TCU);   the host was responsible for all line handling functions (e.g., polling) and error recovery functions and the TCU merely forwarded data from host to terminal and vice versa.

In 1974, IBM announced its architecture for communication networks called Systems Network Architecture (SNA). Initially this architecture was specified for single host systems and VTAM, TCAM and Network Control Program for the 3705 (NCP) were the programs used for implementing the architecture. Later on, the SNA architecture was expanded to support multiple hosts and its implementation was by means of a set of programs called Advanced Functions for Communications (ACF). ACF uses VTAM as its major access method and this variation of VTAM is known as ACF/VTAM. Another access method used by ACF is Telecommunications Access Method (TCAM) and this version of TCAM is known as ACF/TCAM.

To support SNA, the following objectives were added to VTAM:

-   Support new device controllers (e.g., SNA Cluster Controller)

-   Support centralized network host software required by SNA

-   Separation of protocols according to:

    a.   Data Link Protocol

    b.   Device Control Protocol

    c.   End-to-End Protocol

The physical elements of a VTAM environment are the host, communications controller(s), cluster controllers and terminals. Each physical element is called a node. A node contains the following logical elements (i.e., software elements)

o   Logical unit, e.g., application program

o   Physical unit, e.g., a program for performing network functions

In addition, a host node contains a system services control point (SSCP) for performing network management functions. A logical unit (LU), a physical unit (PU) and SSCP are network addressable units (NAUs).

A VTAM network is described hierarchically, using the concept of nodes, and classifying nodes as major or minor. The following are defined as major nodes:

o   Application Programs

o   Communications Controllers (Local and Remote)

o   Sets of Local Terminals

The following are defined as minor nodes:

o   Line Groups

o   Lines

o   Terminals Within a Set.

VTAM uses two modes of communication, namely record
mode and basic mode. The record mode is suitable for
communication in an SNA environment; the basic mode is
for BSC and start/stop terminals.

Data transfer requests can be synchronous or asynchronous. In the synchronous case, VTAM returns control to application program after I/O completion. In the asynchronous case, VTAM returns control to application program
after starting I/O operation.

An application program communicates with VTAM using
macros. Macros are provided for the following purposes:

o   Establishing a connection with VTAM (OPEN)

o   Establishing a connection with a terminal (OPENDST)

o   Communicating with a terminal (SEND/RECEIVE)

o   Disconnecting from a terminal after use (CLSDST)

o   Disconnecting from VTAM (CLOSE)

An application program, in general, executes these macros
in the sequence listed above.

2.9 I/O SUPERVISOR (IOS)

The I/O Supervisor performs initiation and completion of
the I/O operation at a hardware level. It issues the Start
I/O instruction and also handles the interruption arising

from completion of I/O operation. The steps in an I/O operation (with considerable simplification) are listed below:

1. An application program invokes an access method by a GET/PUT or READ/WRITE command.

2. The access method creates channel programs and control blocks for use by IOS.

3. IOS starts the I/O operation by means of START I/O instruction.

4. Control is returned to the access method which puts the application program in a wait state.

5. I/O interrupt handler branches to IOS when it receives an interruption on I/O completion.

6. Assuming the I/O operation was successsful, IOS activates the application program by posting event completion.

2.10 WORKFLOW IN THE OPERATING SYSTEM

We shall give next a simplified description of the task flow and synchronization that is crucial to understanding the overall behavior of the operating system. Figure A-9 presents a flow diagram that illustrates the concepts we have discussed until now. Event 1 shows the dispatcher selecting the highest priority task from a task queue and giving control to the task. The task starts execution and issues an SVC call to start an I/O operation (Event 2). Control passes to the Interruption Handler for handling SVC interruptions and from then on to the I/O Supervisor which performs the Start I/O instruction and puts the task in a wait state (Event 3). The dispatcher continues executing other ready tasks which are not shown in the diagram. When the I/O operation for the first task is complete, an I/O interruption takes place (Event 4) and the I/O Supervisor marks the task as ready for execution by posting event completion (Event 5). The dispatcher resumes execution of the task when its turn comes up, as determined by the priority given to the task.

2.11 MISCELLANEOUS TOPICS

Before application programs can be run, the operating system has to be loaded into the computer system. This process of loading the operating system is known as initialization. An operating system has to be tailored to a particular environment by means of the system generation (SYSGEN) process before it is loaded.

System Generation (SYSGEN). System generation consists of defining the hardware configuration and specifying the selection of operating system modules. Parameters that are specified are exemplified by the following:

o   channel types

o   control unit types

o   device types

o   channel, control unit and device configuration

o   size of real storage

Options specified are of the following types:

o   choice of access methods (BTAM, VTAM, etc.)

o   user written SVC handling routines

o   job entry option

o   time-sharing option

A set of macros are provided for system generation. During system generation, the appropriate macros are selected, their parameters are specified and they are assembled on an existing system. The output of the

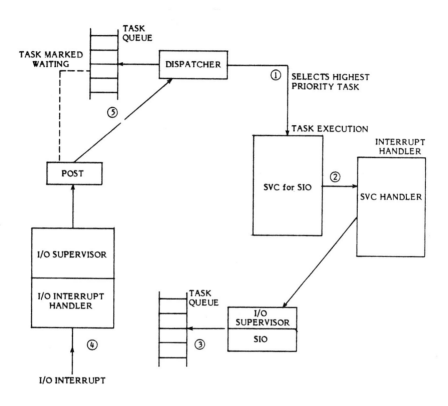

Note: Circled numbers denote events which are described in the text.

Figure A-9/Flow Diagram Showing Task Flow and
Synchronization

system generation process is an MVS operating system tailored to the installation's needs.

Initial Program Loader (IPL). The initial program loader (IPL) is a program that resides on a disk called the system residence volume. IPL is read into main storage when an operator presses the LOAD button on the console panel. IPL clears all general purpose and floating point registers and reads the nucleus created by SYSGEN and written out to the system residence volume. The nucleus is used to invoke various initialization routines that prepare the system for the execution of application programs.

References and Further Reading on MVS

1. OS/VS2 MVS Overview, GC 28-0984-1, May 1980.

2. OS/VS2 MVS System Programming Library: Initialization and Tuning Guide, GC 28-0681-3.

3. OS/VS2 System Logic (7 Volumes) SY 28-0713 through SY 28-0719.

Index